Harriett K. Scarlon

Garrett K. Scanlan

WALKING
AND
TALKING

WALKING AND TALKING:

57 STORIES OF SUCCESS AND HUMOR IN THE REAL ESTATE WORLD OF BUSINESS

GARRETT K. SCANLON

BALLYLONGFORD BOOKS

Copyright© 2006 by Garrett K. Scanlon

Walking and Talking: 57 Stories of Success and Humor in the Real Estate World of Business

All rights reserved. No part of this book may be reproduced in any manner or form whatsoever, by any means, electronically or mechanically, including photocopying or recording, or by any information or retrieval system, without the expressed, written permission from the publisher, except by a reviewer, who may quote brief passages for reviews or articles about the book.

Published by Ballylongford Books, 2588 Welsford Road, Columbus, Ohio 43221.

For additional information or to contact the author: www.walkingandtalking.com. Excerpts are available for reprinting in your publication. Author available for seminars and consulting.

Disclaimer: Readers should always rely on their own legal, accounting and financial counsel in the regards to the purchase, ownership and management of real estate. Any advice contained herein is subject to errors and omissions. Any mention of companies or individuals in this book is not an endorsement of same, and author is not responsible for any real estate investments made by the reader.

Printed and bound in the United States of America.
First printing 2006
ISBN 0-9753612-1-X
1. Real Estate 2. Sales   I. Title   II. Garrett Scanlon.
Cover by Glavan Imageworks

DEDICATION

This book is dedicated to:

Sherri, Michelle and Tony

James and Jeanne Scanlon

Katie, Megan, Jimmy, Kimberly, Kaitlyn, Danny, Michael and Matthew

Randy, Nicole and Riley Wilcox

Bill Ulrich, Tim Kelley, Dave Drake and Doug Jones

Charlie Cavallaro

ACKNOWLEDGMENTS

I would like to thank all of the contributors to *Walking and Talking: 57 Stories of Success and Humor in the Real Estate World of Business*. It has been an honor to be able to spend time, and share stories, with such an impressive and interesting group of people. Your enthusiasm and dedication to your work is very motivating and your knowledge and experience teaches us all. I am very grateful for your help, encouragement and friendship.

To Doug Jones of Triangle Business Systems, you really stepped up to the plate and helped me with this book. But, of course, you've been doing things like that since the fourth grade. It's great that some things never change.

To Julie DeVillers, thank you for your enthusiasm, and for sharing with me your insight and knowledge of writing and publishing.

Thanks to Pat Fay, Jim McGrath, Jeff and Mary Ann Patter, Doris Thomas, Kevin Kelley, Mike Gilliland, Erin Davis, Michael and Kim McShane, Michael and Debbie Jokovich, Melissa Mirenda, Eva Hockenberry, Katie Fox, Janice Webster, and Stefanie Jones who took the time to read the manuscript and provide valuable ideas and feedback.

To the very talented Susan Ledford, thank you for all of your help and creativity.

Thanks to Kristy Stacy and Becky Martzo for all of your help with typesetting, layout and graphic design.

Thanks to Ed Feher, Jeff Glavan, Nathan Adams, and Brett Foster at Glavan Imageworks and Glavan Feher Architects, Inc. for producing the cover of this book.

I am grateful to Don Kelley, Pat Grabill, and Don Kenney for introducing me to the world of real estate.

I am very fortunate to have been greatly influenced by a wonderful family. My wife, Sherri, is one of the most multi-talented people I have ever known, but her most gifted and favorite role is that of loving mother to Michelle and Tony, two young adults who impress us every day with the friends they choose and the choices they make. My parents, James and Jeanne Scanlon, continue to be the two most inspirational people in my life, and my brothers, sisters and in-laws, Mark and Mary Jeanne Evans, Jim and Vicky Scanlon, Dan and Kathy Scanlon, Dave and Kelley Martin, and their children, give every Thanksgiving added meaning.

CONTENTS

Introduction XIV

1. **Stories From Winners in Today's Marketplace**

   Walking and Talking 3
   The Case of the Spiral Notebook 7
   2 Out of 3 Will Save a Tree 9
   Richard's Almanac 11
   Cole's List 14
   A Fortunate Pairing 16

2. **Filed Under "That's Incredible!"**

   You Built Your House on My Lot 29
   Tear Down That House! 35
   The Third Gentleman 37
   I Happened to Read an Article in the Paper 39
   He Really Invested His Money in Land 41
   "You're Looking at a Million Dollar Producer" 42
   What About Bob? 47

3. **Stories of Perspective**

   Keeping Perspective 55
   A Great Start to the Day 57
   Learning to Teach (or Teaching to Learn) 60
   If You Are Going to Do Nothing…Do Nothing Well 62
   Cheese Pies 64
   Planting Flowers 67
   Look What the Wind Blew In 69

4. A Very Special Person

    Nicole Moore Wilcox 73

5. Conversations

    Persistent "Poss" Abilities 80
    In Partnership 83
    Haven't We Had This Conversation Before? 86
    That's Just Not the Standard Way! 88
    Get Out of the Car! 90
    Different Perspectives 92
    Know Your Limits But Don't Limit Your
    Knowledge 95
    Florida Shade 97
    The Three-Two Pitch 100
    All in the Family 103
    Walking the Hall Way 105
    You Ought to be an Architect! 107

6. Stories of Risk and Reward

    7 11 12 14 28 32 116
    5 14 17 35 36 41 120
    Easy Street? 122
    Pull! 124
    Meeting Mrs. Claus 127
    Dealing with Uncertainty 129

7. Stories of Technology

    I Have Carried a Computer in My Pocket for 20 Years! 134
    Knowing Technology (Yours & Theirs) 137
    It Was 4%...Do You Copy? 139
    With the Touch of a Button 141

8. Developing Stories

Get a Hobby! 146
You Can Always Do What You Do Not Want to Do 149
Good Advice Is Timeless 152
Green Acres 155
If You Don't Buy It, I Will! 158
Tomorrow Morning, Wake Up 20 Years from Now 162
Emergency Phone Call! 166

9. A Second Set of Footprints

It's All About Timing 170
Let's Skip to Another Story 172
Eight is Enough 174
The Get-Rich-Slow Method 176
He Was Evicted, to His Good Fortune 178
Coach Pedon 180
Choices Made and Big Shoes To Fill 183

10. Notes, Quotes and Asides

Quotes and Asides from the People
"Walking and Talking" 190

  Afterword
  About the Author

INTRODUCTION

"Uncle Garry, do you want to read me a story?" my two-year-old nephew blurted out. Before I had a chance to respond, he was flying off the couch and racing toward a pile of books. He returned with one of his favorites, which I read to him in just a few short minutes. "Again!" he demanded. So back we went to page one. This time I added more inflection to the "mooooos," the "quacks," and the "baaas." Truly a riveting performance! "Again! Again!" he cried. I knew where this was headed.

So I asked him, "Michael, why don't you tell me a story?" Back we went to page one. He was too young to read, but not too young to tell a story. He created his own story about a horse that jumped "really high" and a dog that ran "really fast." And his big finish was "Theeeee end." That story he "read" to me that day remains one of my personal favorites.

Stories have been a part of all of our lives since we were children. We connect to a good story. This became very clear to me while teaching a class titled "Understanding the Fundamentals of Investment Real Estate." The class is a discussion of real estate cash flow, appreciation, construction, property management, tax deferral, and other topics. Attendees include real estate brokers, lenders, and investors in Columbus, Ohio. The class response is always more positive when real life stories are included as examples to the topics being discussed. Practical stories make the subject more relevant, more entertaining, more memorable.

Some of the people featured in this book are ultra-successful. Most of the people, however, are in the category of achievers who have reached a very high, yet attainable level of business success.

They haven't won the lottery (well, actually, one of them did). They are hardworking people who continually look for ways to succeed, year in and year out, in a very competitive environment. They are some of the most talented and interesting people winning in today's business world. And you will read their stories. Some stories are inspiring, some educational, some funny, some insightful. The stories can spark new ideas to assist you in your own business ventures. They can motivate you and entertain you. I hope you will enjoy them all.

1

Stories From Winners In Today's Marketplace

Walking and Talking

Stories From Winners In Today's Marketplace

WALKING AND TALKING

Ronald Reagan was just starting his second term as president when I began a career in investment real estate. I joined a group of 25 real estate agents with Coldwell Banker Commercial Real Estate in Columbus, Ohio. It was a very friendly and ambitious group of people, eager like me, to make a career in commercial real estate. One of those agents was Wayne Harer.

Wayne Harer played ten years of minor league baseball for the Red Sox and Yankee organizations. Wayne had the distinction of winning the International League's AAA batting title with a .350 batting average. Unfortunately, Boston's outfield consisted of American League MVP's Freddie Lynn and Jim Rice, and Hall of Famer Carl Yastrzemski. I considered Wayne a veteran in the business because he had all of two years experience leasing downtown office space.

One day, Wayne was walking through our office lobby. "Hey Wayne," I called. "Could I ask you a couple of questions?"

"Walk with me, talk with me!" was his reply. Huh? As Wayne got on the elevator he repeated, "Walk with me, talk with me! Let's go!" Being new in the business, I jumped at the invita-

3

tion. Not only was Wayne a successful sales agent, he was the only guy I knew who had his own baseball card!

I spent the next two hours tagging along with Wayne as he conducted business downtown. He visited a dozen offices, dropping off brochures, asking to talk with the tenants and owners. A business card handed out here, a "Howyabeen" there. We took elevators and escalators; we cut across parking lots and through retail stores. I kept asking Wayne real estate questions. Wayne kept walking and talking. Five miles later, it was obvious that Wayne knew every floor of every downtown building, every owner, and every tenant. He knew everyone by name: the secretaries, the lobby clerks, even the policemen on the corner. You were never a stranger for long when "Wayno" was walking and talking.

"When I was hired by Coldwell Banker they said, 'You are going to be an office broker.' That sounded great to me, but I really didn't know what they meant by that," Wayne recalls.

"When I asked them what exactly an office broker did, they pointed outside their office window and said, 'Do you see all of those buildings out there? You are going to learn everything there is to know about every single floor of every single building.' They told me I needed to meet with every tenant, leasing agent, property manager, lender and owner associated with those buildings; that I needed to find out all of the square footages, the rental incentives being offered, the type of tenant improvements being done and the details of every lease being signed downtown. That can seem like a daunting task for a new real estate agent, fresh out of professional baseball. It took me about 18 months to do that groundwork. And it is groundwork! Your energy level has to be very high. When you start at the top of the LeVeque Tower and start working, floor by floor, it can be exhausting."

However, as someone who has reached the pinnacle of his profession, Wayne explains, "There is no substitute for personal canvassing. You learn so much more from visiting an office location than you can from a phone call. You might see office workers packed into very small space, telling you they need to expand. Or maybe the opposite is true and there are 4 people walking around in 5,000 square feet of space. They might need to sub-lease some of their space to cut overhead. Is their office too hot in July or too cold in December? Maybe you notice a leak in the ceiling or maybe you hear one of the secretaries complain that the property management company doesn't respond to maintenance concerns. All these things help you recognize the particular needs and requirements of tenants."

I remember the time someone asked Wayne, "What if there is a *no solicitation* sign outside the office?" Wayne replied, "Better yet! That means there is a good chance all of the other brokers were scared off. The reality is, if you haven't been thrown out of every building in your territory at least once, then you're not doing your job."

As of early 2005, the major issue for tenants choosing office space became one of human resources. According to Wayne, "Business owners' main emphasis when choosing space is how it will affect their ability to hire talented professionals. Today, they value the building-design, parking, prestige and location of office space in terms of how they can use their office space to lure employees from competing businesses and/or from other areas of town. Before, their only consideration had to do with their customers. Now they want their office to attract the best personnel; the best sales agents, attorneys, financial planners, architects, etc. to their company."

As his business expands, Wayne schedules luncheons with members of development departments and chambers of commerce. He gives presentations to small groups of brokers, company executives and building-owners. He has built a "team" of space planners, tenant improvement contractors, legal and financial analysts, and marketing specialists to provide service to those clients with whom he still gets face-to-face.

The questions I had for Wayne were insignificant compared to the education he gave me that day: walking and talking. This is what it is all about. Getting face-to-face and personal with the people with whom you want to do business. He not only became familiar with the product, inside and out, but also grew to know the individuals who would later become his customers. Certainly, there were scores of agents "working the phones," making calls to potential clients, but there is no substitute for meeting face-to-face the way that Wayne Harer demonstrated.

Today, Wayne still sports 2 AAA World Championship Rings from his days with the Columbus Clippers in the early 80s. You can watch him announcing televised games for the Clippers, coaching his kid's little league games and running an occasional marathon. Wayne, now with Continental Real Estate, has been honored in 5 of the last 6 years as the Highest Volume Commercial Sales Leader in Columbus, averaging over $70 million of volume per year…walking and talking.

Stories From Winners In Today's Marketplace

THE CASE OF THE SPIRAL NOTEBOOK

Chuck Manofsky immediately drew my attention when he said, "If you do this, I guarantee it will someday, somehow make you money." Chuck is an outstanding leader, who, as Director of Asset Services for CB Richard Ellis, manages a large portfolio of Midwest office buildings. I wanted to know his secrets.

Chuck asked me if I was using a spiral notebook. I replied, "What for?" Chuck reached back to his credenza, grabbed a 5" x 7.5" spiral notebook and tossed it across his desk to me.

"Use this to jot down notes from your phone calls."

I replied, "Oh, I sometimes use a yellow pad for that."

Chuck just rolled his eyes. "Use the spiral notebook," he said, "for calls you make, and for calls you receive. Write every call down. If someone calls to tell you your car was towed, write it down. If you call a friend, write it down. Develop a habit of keeping notes on every call you make or take and write down the phone numbers so you will have easy reference for creating your 'to-do' lists."

Chuck told me he earned a sizable commission as a result of referring to information he had written in his spiral pad. And then he said, "If you do this, I guarantee it will someday, somehow make you money." I took the spiral notebook.

A few years later, a friend of mine asked me for an opinion about an office building he wanted to purchase. He asked if the sale price was reasonable, and if the building's leases truly reflected the market rate for office space in the area. After researching the building and verifying the projected net operating income, I obtained sales data for other comparable properties that had sold, and told him that it appeared to be a great property at a great price.

Three weeks later, I offhandedly asked if he planned to buy the building and was surprised when he answered that he had already purchased it. In fact, a broker who represented a potential buyer for the building had already contacted him. He was going to resell the building! In light of the research I had done, I asked to be given first crack at locating a buyer. He agreed to give me until Friday afternoon. It was Wednesday morning.

So there I sat at my desk, wondering how to sell a $16 million dollar office building in two days.

It was then that I decided to go to the spiral notebook. Five minutes later, there it was scribbled in my notes: the name of a qualified buyer who had called two months earlier, asking me to keep an eye out for large office buildings with strong leases. It prompted me to remember our previous conversations and his claim that he would act very quickly if a good opportunity came along. I called him regarding the available building, and he did indeed act quickly.

The next day, he faxed a contract. Two months later we closed the sale. I gained my commission and my own story about the spiral notepad. Chuck Manofsky will tell you, if you use one too, it will give you a good story as well!

2 OUT OF 3 WILL SAVE A TREE

New Year's Day I immediately started following through on my resolution to get organized. After another busy holiday season, it was time to clean house and plan strategies for a brand new year. I reviewed each file, kept what was relevant, and tossed out the rest. Closed files, In-Contract files, Miscellaneous files. Files, files, files!

Then onward to my desk! I continued to keep the files that still had some potential and threw away the ones that were only taking up needed space. Next up, the vertical file on top of my credenza. Same thing; out with the old stuff and in with the new!

After organizing, paring down and tossing away files, I was stunned by what I saw. On the floor, leading all the way from my desk to the office door, were wastebaskets full of files. I wanted to go outside and plant a tree just to replace the tree on my office floor. The remaining 'relevant' folders could almost fit in my briefcase!

WOW! Major epiphany. More than half of everything I had worked on the previous year was ultimately unproductive.

Walking and Talking

Wouldn't it be fantastic if we could somehow identify those activities destined to be successful and avoid the others? Think of how productive we would become with the freed-up time! The problem is, we've all seen improbable deals that actually work out! Everyone has a story of an unusual deal or an unexpected stroke of good fortune that ended with a great result. And much of our success comes from being optimistic.

However, glancing once again at my overflowing wastebasket reminded me to limit the time I spend on opportunities with marginal probabilities for success, and to spend more time on projects that have the best chance of closing.

This brings us to Ed Joseph of CB Richard Ellis, Inc. Somehow, Ed always manages to avoid those huge stacks of files at year's end. Yet there he is, year after year, leading the way with outstanding sales volume. Nobody has sold as much multifamily property in Central Ohio over the last 20 years as Ed Joseph. Yet he never looks busy! Ed's ability to focus on deals that succeed, and avoid wasting time on those that do not, makes him a perennial sales leader. How does he do it?

Before Ed commits his time and effort in a particular direction, he asks himself these three questions:

1. How much time and effort will the project require?
2. Is the probability for success very high or very low?
3. If he is successful, how well will he be compensated?

If at least 2 of the 3 are in his favor, Ed gets to work! If not, Ed remains disciplined enough to walk away. I always remember this philosophy as: 2 out of 3 will save a tree.

Stories From Winners In Today's Marketplace

RICHARD'S ALMANAC

Is it just by chance that Richard Schuen, president of Grubb & Ellis/Adena Realty Advisors has become one of today's most successful and talented brokers in Ohio? I contend that it was inevitable.

That is a strong word. Inevitable. But haven't we all, at one time or another, observed someone at a very early stage in their career, doing things so well and with such determination, perseverance and planning, that their success seemed inevitable? Richard is one of those people who destined himself to success.

Generally, they are great people to emulate from a professional standpoint, and usually they are wonderful people with whom to share good friendships. We had both just begun our careers in commercial real estate selling multifamily investment property, when I met Richard 20 years ago. The price of $3.95 for the soup and salad bar at the YWCA downtown fit our budget, and we tried to make use of the athletic club nearby.

Richard, who had been a great athlete in high school and college, shared with me what seemed like an almost bizarre theory. He believed you had to stay in shape physically to per-

Walking and Talking

form at your best professionally. He and I were in our late 20's when he made mention of this, and staying in shape seemed relatively easy at the time. I never considered eating the right foods and getting plenty of sleep and exercise as determinants in earning a living in real estate. What did writing contracts, locating available properties, and brokering deals have to do with those things anyway?

Richard, of course, was absolutely right. He had developed a warrior-type attitude towards reaching his goals. The world of real estate is a very competitive environment and staying as physically fit as possible is part of the equation. Still, I was having difficulty accepting his premise, until he said, "You can be the best salesman in the world, but if you continually let yourself get run down, there isn't much you can do if you are in bed with the flu."

He could have very well added, "or tired in the mornings, or low on energy throughout the day, or not as confident when working with others who have balance in their life." Richard was not the first person to think of this concept. Two hundred years ago, in his popular periodical titled Poor Richard's Almanac, Benjamin Franklin detailed at length, the importance of adding discipline to your personal life to succeed in your career. Richard Schuen, implements this concept as well as anyone I have ever known.

As a volunteer teacher for Junior Achievement, I have taught young kids how to save and invest, how to interview for jobs and prepare financially for their future. I tell them, however, that the most dramatic way in which they can improve their odds for success is to avoid alcohol, drugs and tobacco, to exercise, eat right and add balance to their life. It almost seems too simplistic to even discuss. Discussing these simple disciplines, however, helps to remind them, and me, how important it is to make them a priority in our lives.

Dr. William B. Malarkey, Director of The Ohio State University Clinical Research Center and Professor of Internal Medicine and Endocrinology has written a very interesting and practical book on this subject titled Take Control of Your Aging. In his book he describes how the PIERS of our lives can add foundation and prevent erosion in our lives. PIERS is an acronym for Physical, Intellectual, Emotional, Relational and Spiritual. I highly recommend it to anyone interested in taking control of their aging, their career and their personal life.

From Benjamin Franklin to Richard Schuen, some truths never change!

COLE'S LIST

Cole Ellis grew up in Lima, Ohio, attended The Ohio State University, married his wife Michele, moved to Columbus, rented an apartment, walked into my office, introduced himself and said he was eager to join our company and sell investment real estate.

Cole spent the next two years of his life living and breathing real estate. He did all of the right things. He was a great communicator and he leveraged this ability by talking with everyone in sight. He soon learned the dynamics of real estate and demonstrated the product knowledge of a 20-year veteran. Despite all of this, his first year was slow. Then came year two, but it was slow as well.

The most talented people I have ever seen in this industry have usually taken two to three years to hit their stride. In his third year, Cole became one of the highest volume agents in Columbus. He even sold me my first four-family building!

I kept asking Cole if the building he was selling me was overpriced. "No!" he said, "The rents will improve, interest rates are good, and there are only two buildings left for sale in the area." He sold me!

A month later Cole came in my office and asked if he should buy the last remaining building next to mine. "Sure, Cole," I said, "Rates are good, rents are going up." Cole replied, "Yeah, but that price seems too high." We both looked up and stared at each other for a couple seconds, then burst out laughing. Cole bought the building.

One day I walked into Cole's office to suggest that he call two lenders who might be able to send some business his way. A few minutes later, when I was leaving his office, I realized he had not written down the idea of calling the lenders.

I said, "Don't forget to call those two guys!"

Cole replied, "O.K., I'll call them," but he still didn't write it down on paper.

"Aren't you going to write that down on your to-do list?" I asked.

"I don't keep a to-do list. I'll just call them, right now, as soon as you leave," he said.

I could not believe it. Here was one of the busiest agents in town with dozens of things to do each day, and he didn't keep a to-do list?! It seemed impossible!

He said, "No. I keep a day planner for appointments. The other things I just do."

And then it occurred to me that I had never seen Cole with a legal pad with the typical pages and pages of items. Cole never waits to do anything. Cole just does it. He doesn't talk about doing it. He doesn't plan on doing it. He doesn't prioritize it above or below other activities. He just does it. Since then, whenever I begin to write down a "to-do" activity, I first try to put it on "Cole's List" and just do it!

Today Cole owns Ellis Companies and Buckeye Self Storage and develops multi-use investment property.

A FORTUNATE PAIRING

On a sunny day in 1998, Bob Hoying decided to play a quick round of golf, threw his clubs in his car and drove to Heritage Golf Club. There he was introduced to and paired with another golfer, Brent Crawford. They discovered that both of them were from small towns, were the same age, and both had graduated from The Ohio State University in 1995. However, the paths they took through college were very different from each other.

Brent Crawford arrived from Batavia, Ohio, near Cincinnati to be a communications major at OSU. His sophomore year, along with some friends, he rented a house near campus.

Brent recalls, "Our landlord was Mark Mayers, who incidentally is now our Chief Operating Officer. I observed how well he was doing, renting that house to us. Mark was a great mentor to me and explained how I could get started in real estate. However, like a lot of other students, I didn't have money for a downpayment on a house."

"So, I borrowed $1,500 from my girlfriend's grandmother to buy my first house. The price was $70,000. It had 4 bedrooms and 1 bath."

"Some girlfriend!" I said.

Brent smiled. "You bet. She's my wife now; Liz. I rented it to five of my buddies and I lived there myself. Basically, I ended up living there for free. Three months later I purchased another house. Over the next year, I purchased another ten homes."

All the while, Brent worked part-time at Nationwide Insurance as a claims representative and took a full course-load at school.

"Liz and I managed the apartments ourselves. We would gut the apartments down to the studs, if necessary. We did everything. The landscaping, the siding; whatever was needed. It was a matter of learning on the job. We took any positive cash flow and plowed it back into the properties. After fixing-up the first two properties, we had them re-appraised at the improved value and refinanced them. There was enough money left over, after paying off the original loan, for us to use as a downpayment for the next purchase," Brent says.

Brent recalls one day visiting one of his favorite teachers from high school, Gary Sroufe.

"I mentioned to Gary that I had bought a few homes and he suggested we go in as partners on the purchase of several more homes. We structured our agreement so that Gary would supply the downpayment and I would perform all of the physical work. I located the properties, arranged the financing, and performed the property management. Out of the cash flow, we first paid Gary a return on his downpayment. Everything after that, the appreciation, principal reduction, and added cash flow, was split 50-50."

By the time Brent graduated, he owned 30 units, consisting of single family homes and duplexes. Because he purchased the property at good prices and rehabbed each property, his real estate greatly increased in value. However, Brent considered campus property to be extremely management intensive, so he sold the property and, with the proceeds, purchased 5 sixteen-family buildings at Pine Lake/Saddlebrook Apartments.

Soon thereafter is when Brent was paired for golf with Bob Hoying.

Bob Hoying always acts surprised when I remind him that one of the things we have in common is that both of us are natural athletes. Bob played quarterback and free safety at St. Henry High School and was named Ohio Mr. Football in1990. That same year, I pitched 8 complete softball games for Plank's Cafe and led the team in walks.

As quarterback for The Ohio State Buckeyes, Bob completed more career passes than any other OSU quarterback and set the record for most touchdown passes in a game (5), a season (29) and a career (57). Senior year, Bob won the Draddy Trophy, considered the "academic" Heisman Trophy, presented by the National Football Foundation and College Hall of Fame. In the actual Heisman Trophy competition, Bob placed 10th in the balloting, behind Peyton Manning (6th), Danny Wuerffel (3rd), and teammate Eddie George, who won the award. During that same period of time, I crowded the plate and was hit-by-a-pitch 7 times. These are statistics that can be verified.

Bob's favorite honor, however, was being named co-captain his senior year at OSU along with Eddie George. "That was a particularly special honor because the selection was made by my teammates," Bob says.

After being voted MVP of the 1996 Senior Bowl, a game that featured a record 81 NFL draftees, Bob was drafted by the Philadelphia Eagles. Bob became starting quarterback in midseason of 1997 and threw for 11 touchdown passes by the end of the year, including 3 in a memorable 44-42 win over Boomer Esiason and the Cincinnati Bengals. False rumors of a bad knee kept me out of professional sports.

But throughout his 7-year NFL career, Bob kept considering which career path he would take after football.

Although Brent and Bobby did not discuss real estate or football during that first round of golf together, they eventually compared notes and decided to team-up in the field of real estate. A couple of years later they purchased Gateway Lakes, a 252 unit apartment community. Within another two years, they acquired over 2,000 apartments, and by 2006 they increased that number to 8,000.

For Bob Hoying, real estate is a natural fit. "I feel very fortunate to have found something that I love to do. It is difficult for a lot of players to make that transition into another field after their sports career ends. More than anything else, from my days in the NFL, I miss the camaraderie shared by the players. To a great extent, however, you see that same need for teamwork in real estate. When you and your colleagues are working on a project, everyone is using their particular expertise to achieve a common goal."

According to Brent, "Since we formed our company 7 years ago, Bob and I have not had a single disagreement. The reason is neither of us needs to have our own way. Both of us are willing to give and take. And we compliment each other very well. I tend to be very aggressive and always look at the big picture of things. Bob is more conservative and detail oriented, making sure that we are growing in a disciplined fashion. He oversees development and construction, along with his brother Tom, which right now includes the building of high-end homes priced between $800,000 and $1.3 million dollars. I focus more on acquisitions and property management. You need to have both of those dynamics working together like that."

And Bob explains that it is important to have fun along the way. "My dad has been in the construction business for a long time and he has always emphasized that you should work hard and have fun. If you think about it, you can apply that principle to about everything you do. You certainly have to put forth the time and effort, but that isn't worth anything unless you enjoy what you do. What I most like is taking a project from a piece of ground all the way through final completion. It's exciting to look back, after 12 months of hard work on a development project, and see the success you ultimately hoped would occur."

According to Bob, "There are a lot of factors that must come together for a project to succeed. Brent and I consider ourselves cautiously aggressive. We have made it our strategy to surround ourselves with good people, continue to grow, and limit our mistakes to small ones."

Crawford and Hoying have vertically integrated their operations and currently employ 250 people. They now own companies that provide property management, title insurance, brokerage, landscaping, painting, cleaning, carpet replacement, building and maintenance supplies, property and casualty insurance and, with the formation of Brackett Builders Inc., new construction.

I asked Brent what has been the best real estate advice he has received. He replied, "Early on, during those campus years, Mark Mayers always emphasized that money is worthless if you don't have a reputation of honesty and integrity. And it is so true. When we are sitting around the conference table working on our various deals, money is the last consideration that comes into the picture. We like earning money, don't get me wrong, but our first consideration is whether or not it is the right thing to do."

Brent and Bob applied this same attitude when they joined in the relief effort in the aftermath of Hurricane Katrina.

Brent recalls, "Like everyone else, we were watching things unfold on television, and saw the devastation down there. Our first reaction was to donate money to help out. But when you do that, you always wonder if it will be spent correctly or if it will just go to waste. So we decided to take more direct action."

The next day they held a strategy meeting. Brent and Bob, along with their wives Liz and Jill, decided they wanted to make a significant impact on the lives of some of the people devastated from the hurricane. As Brent explains, "We felt that if we made short-term arrangements for the families, they would not receive long-term benefits." With that in mind, they developed criteria for the type of individuals they could most assist.

Brent recalls. "We were looking for people who 1.) Had lost absolutely everything, 2.) Had children, 3.) Had been employed and wished to continue to work. Dave and Jenny Whinham were instrumental in the process. Dave's brother worked in Louisiana and knew the area well and they actually went to the shelters to handpick a family needing help."

They found a family of 25, consisting of 6 sisters, 1 brother, and their children. Within a few days, they located their father, who had become separated and was in West Virginia, their mother who had been sent to a shelter in Alabama, and the 6th sister and her husband, who had fled to Texas.

"You cannot imagine how big of an operation it is to relocate that many people, especially when you are thinking long-term," Brent says. "There were so many issues to deal with; housing, furniture, food, clothing, transportation, health insurance, school, and medical issues. One couple actually had a baby one week after arrival. I was so impressed with everyone with our company. They were literally working 17-hour days for a couple of weeks."

By Tuesday of the following week, Brent and Bob's secretary Dawn Russell and her husband Joe, a firefighter, along with a nurse, a police officer, and a minister, rode a custom coach packed full of relief supplies donated by the Upper Arlington Lutheran Church, to New Orleans. They unloaded the supplies to the shelter and picked up the families for the long drive north to Columbus, Ohio.

The Crawford Hoying organization of friends, family and business colleagues came together to relocate a grand total of 35 men, women, and children. 31 had never been outside of Louisiana! Various churches and individuals provided clothes, food, bibles, toys, appliances, pots and pans, diapers and more. Steve Germain donated 9 brand new Toyota Corollas on two-year leases for free. One donor contributed one full year of free health care for everyone. Village Academy in Powell contributed greatly to the entire operation. Crawford Hoying provided 9 completely furnished apartments, with free rent and utilities for 1 year. Most importantly, 10 of the adults were provided jobs at Crawford Hoying. The families from New Orleans, however, were provided a hand-up, not a handout.

"This is not about getting things back to where they were," Brent says. "The goal is to provide them with opportunities to make their lives better than the ones they had before. This is why we picked this particular family. They all want to continue to work and are appreciative of the opportunity. They work in a variety of jobs including leasing, construction, maintenance, and grounds. Some have that background of experience, others were cooks. But the standard of living was so low in New Orleans that, even with both parents working, they were still not able to make ends meet."

Within 2 weeks of arrival, Liz Crawford had helped to enroll all of the children in schools and scheduled doctor's appointments for those needing medical attention. She had her fellow photography students at the Dublin Arts Center spend a day taking photographs of the families to replace all of the family photos that had been destroyed in the flood.

"We have all become friends throughout this process," Brent says. "Their kids like their schools and everyone is making friends and fitting into the community. It is certainly the greatest feeling of accomplishment we've ever experienced, including any we have had in our business. To see them all gather in one of our apartment clubhouses this year, celebrating Thanksgiving together, was great to see."

But Brent and Bob explain that this is only the beginning. The next goal is to arrange college funding for all of the kids. And, along the way, they want each family to make the transition from apartment rental to home ownership.

"They really intend on making Columbus their home," says Bob.

Anyone interested in helping the cause can contact The Crawford Hoying Foundation.

To this day, Brent and Bob do not seem to agree on who shot a lower round of golf that summer day, a few years back, but the families from Katrina must undoubtedly agree that, regardless of who shot the lowest round, it was certainly a fortunate pairing.

Walking and Talking

2

Filed Under "That's Incredible!"

Walking and Talking

Filed Under "That's Incredible!"

> *"How often have I said to you that when you have eliminated the impossible, whatever remains however improbable, must be the truth."*
>
> *Sherlock Holmes*

There are many interesting and unusual happenings that occur in the exciting world of real estate. In this chapter they are **Filed Under "That's Incredible!"**

When I think of such happenings, I am reminded of the buyer who had unrealistic cash flow expectations from an investment property she was about to buy.

Years earlier, she and her husband had invested in land that had subsequently appreciated in value. After her husband passed away and she had sold the land to a single-family homebuilder, she decided to use the proceeds from that sale to buy income-producing apartments.

With a wonderful smile, she looked across the closing table and asked, "Now Garry, explain to me again how much cash flow I should expect from this investment."

We had discussed this earlier at length, and I replied, "Again, it is only an estimate, but your cash flow should range somewhere between $7,000 and $8,000."

"That's right," she said. "Now, should I expect that same amount *every* year?"

I was incredulous. Surely, we couldn't have come this far without having communicated a clearer understanding of her return-on-investment. "No," I responded. "That will be your *monthly* cash flow."

She raised her eyebrows and dropped her jaw. In disbelief, she turned to her real estate agent seated at her right and asked, "Is that right?"

He replied that it was indeed her anticipated **monthly** cash flow. She looked around the table to see if there was some mistake. She then looked at me again and asked, "So, what you're telling me is that I could essentially retire?"

Throughout the rest of the closing, we were simply going through the motions. We had all just experienced the pleasure of watching someone realize their investment dream right before our eyes. Years of real estate investment had suddenly culminated in a life-changing event.

Following are other incredible stories…

Filed Under "That's Incredible!"

YOU BUILT YOUR HOUSE ON MY LOT!

I was at my sister's house one Sunday afternoon enjoying a family cookout when my brother Jim said, "You know, you ought to interview Ron Moss for your book."

"Why is that?" I asked.

Jim laughed. "Well unusual things just seem to happen to Ron."

My ears perked up. As a SWAT officer for the Columbus Division of Police, my brother has had his share of unusual happenings. So, if Jim was saying that about Ron Moss, I knew there had to be a good story.

"For instance," Jim said, "He has been shot in the head on two different occasions, and survived."

It was slowly occurring to me that I had never met anyone who had survived one shot to the head, more less two, when Jim said, "But for your book, Ron was once approached by a guy in his front yard who explained that Ron's house was built by mistake on another person's lot."

As I was writing down Ron's number, Jim added, "Oh, and ask him about the time his boat sank and he was lost at sea."

Walking and Talking

After 25 years with the Columbus Police Division, SWAT officer Ron Moss still has the imposing presence of a person who regularly lifts weights and takes physical conditioning very seriously. Because Ron's father was a pastor with the Church of the Nazarene, Ron's family relocated every 7 years to different churches in different states including Michigan, Indiana and eventually New Jersey, where he first met his wife.

It was off the coast of Fortescue, New Jersey, where Ron, in July of 1992, set off for a day of fishing with his younger brother Calvin and their friend, 69-year-old Herb Trout. True to his name, Herb was an avid fisherman who had fished with the Moss brothers on several occasions. They left the marina early in the morning anticipating a great day.

"The weather was beautiful," Ron recalls. "We were drift-fishing. This is where you turn off the boat's engine and drift with the ocean currents. Inevitably, the other boats in the area, that are also drifting, cluster close to each other. Each time this happens, everyone compares notes, and that particular day every boat was bringing in a lot of fish. One guy remarked that they had caught a couple of sharks, but by and large everyone was fishing for flounder, sea bass and sea trout."

Ron says, "At 3 o'clock in the afternoon, the waves started picking up. Herb, a World War II veteran who had fought in the Navy, said, 'Boys, reel it up! We're going home!' I remember him saying that to us, like it was yesterday. Herb went to start the engine, but this time it didn't start. Can you imagine that? We had stopped and started that engine a dozen times that day with no problems. Anyway, Herb went to work cleaning off the spark plugs and even dismantling parts of the engine.

At about that time it began to rain. We looked all around us, and suddenly realized that all of the boats had left for shore. One last boat was passing by some distance away, so we signaled our distress horn, but they didn't hear us over the noise of their boat engines, blasting for home. The rain was getting heavier and Herb was having no success with the engine. Calvin asked, 'Shouldn't we get on the radio and call someone?' None of us had cell phones back then. As it turned out, this was Herb's first time out on his boat all season and the radio was not hooked up. We were six miles off the coast and were beginning to drift out of the bay into the ocean. We placed the anchor in the water at a shallow depth of just a few feet to slow our boat down. The waves continued to get rougher and rougher, when, without any warning at all, a huge wave drenched our boat."

"Calvin yelled out, 'Hey, we're sinking!' It all happened so fast. We literally had only a few seconds to decide what to grab before jumping into the water. We took two life preservers, a seat cushion, the cooler, and a flair gun I saw sitting on the steering console. The Coast Guard later confirmed that the water temperature was between 59 and 61 degrees. And there wasn't a single boat nearby. We emptied the cooler of fish (they call that chumming Ron) and held onto it as a floatation device. That kept us all together. After a couple of hours we considered trying to swim to shore, but the waves were so high that there was no visibility in any direction. We wouldn't have known which way to go, and battling those waves would have been fruitless. The guys with the Coast Guard said that, at that point, we were nearing our half-way point of succumbing to exposure. Fortunately we had kept our hats on which helped us retain some body heat."

Ron recalled the words of the fisherman who had reported earlier that day catching a couple of sharks, and radio accounts of a big white shark that had been caught in the cape a few weeks earlier. To worsen matters, the flare gun had slipped out of Ron's pocket, and Herb had become unresponsive from the exposure.

We'll come back to this story, but this is, after all, a real estate book.

"So Ron, what about building your house on someone else's lot?" I asked.

"Oh that!" he replied. "I was outside walking my dog when some guy I'd never seen in my life walked into the middle of my wife's flower garden and said, 'Hey, you got a problem!' Now you have to understand, I have to get permission from my wife to remove a weed from that garden, and here this guy is trampling through the flowers saying I have a problem? I was thinking, buddy, you are the one with a problem! Anyway, he rolls out this plot plan that shows that my house is located on my neighbor's land, land that he says he is going to buy. Initially, I thought he just wanted me to pay for a survey he needed to obtain for his financing. We had lived in the house for 10 years and I couldn't imagine how we could have built it on the wrong lot. We had obtained a survey for our construction loan, our permanent loan and then once again when we refinanced at lower interest rates."

"But when I checked with the county recorder's office, sure enough, they double-checked the deed and told me that I was wrong; that my house was on my neighbor's lot. After my calls to the title insurance company went largely unanswered, I contacted an attorney who suggested that I meet with the surveyor. The surveyor immediately detected the problem. He said, 'They left out the part that says, starting 185 feet from the pin. That omission causes the wrong starting point, which throws off all of the results.' So, I did own the land beneath my house after all."

I said to Ron, "So, Jim tells me you've been shot on a couple of occasions."

"Yes," he said.

Sensing my hope for a just a little more elaboration, he continued, "One time, my guardian angel must have been working through my partner at the time, Gary Rundio, because he saved my life. We were working narcotics and it was supposed to be an easy night. Nothing very important was planned for that day. Unexpectedly, we were given information about the whereabouts of a drug and gun dealer who had threatened to kill cops if they ever came after him. We set up a reconnaissance plan to raid the premises and we were ready to go, when Rundio told me, 'Dress up!'"

I resisted the urge to tell Ron about the time I got into a scuffle with my best friend in 8th grade because he had made fun of my tennis shoes, and asked, "What's 'dress up' mean?"

"Basically he meant putting on a vest and a helmet. Today it is mandatory to wear them when you are on a raid, but back then it was optional. I would just wear a regular baseball cap that identified me as a police officer. Helmets somewhat restrict your vision and they were only supposed to be able to stop a .22 or light shrapnel anyway. Drug dealers never use a .22 handgun. So what was the point?"

"But Rundio was emphatic. He said, 'Just wear it!'. I even think he threw the helmet at me. As we approached the door to the premises, just by chance, a doorman opened the door to let someone out. He yelled, 'Five-0! Five-0!'. When I entered, the suspect raised a 9mm Glock 17 and fired it at me."

The bullet hit a rivet in Ron's helmet, saving his life.

Ron rubbed the side of his head. "That rivet felt like a hot poker. I can still feel where that bullet hit."

Ron had to leave for another meeting, so the specifics of the second shooting will have to wait for Walking and Talking Some More, but Ron's experience in the waters off the Eastern Coast ended with a happy result.

After 3 hours in the water and no boat in sight, it continued to rain and the water was still choppy. I asked Ron if, at that point, he questioned whether or not he would survive.

Walking and Talking

"There was never a doubt in my mind that we would survive. I had no anxiety or fear that we wouldn't make it. We just kept our minds focused on what we had to do to keep going."

Surprised, I asked, "Well, what do you do when you're lost 6 miles off shore, treading water for 3 hours? Do you pray a lot?"

Ron smiled, "Well, I'm sure we probably did, but like my father always said, 'If you're prayed up in advance, you don't need to worry about that.'"

While treading water, Ron had no way of knowing that, hours earlier, a sail boat had diverted off-course to take refuge from the storm in the Delaware Bay. By good fortune, or by yet another protective act by Ron's guardian angel, you decide, the shortest person on the boat was at the wheel.

"It was her turn at the wheel," Ron recalls. "Because she was so short, they had a box for her to stand on. That box actually placed her eye-level above those of the other people on the boat. She kept saying, 'I see something. I'm sure of it.' The others couldn't see us, but after following her direction they found us and called the Coast Guard who retrieved us from the water."

"Probably because of the adrenalin, I didn't even feel the cold until we were rescued and I was back home. Then, I was colder than I had ever been in my life; just cold to the core. It took me a long time to get warm again."

All three men survived. Herb Trout decided to retire from fishing those waters, and Calvin followed the footsteps of his older brother and is now a police officer in Baltimore Maryland.

And unusual things, no doubt, continue to happen to Ron Moss.

Filed Under "That's Incredible!"

TEAR DOWN THAT HOUSE!

It didn't take long for sign companies to realize that the third generation of The Weiler Co. was going to make a big impact on Ohio real estate. I once asked Skip Weiler who makes more profit: his real estate investors or his sign company? It sometimes seems as if you cannot turn a corner in Columbus without driving past one of his "For Sale or Lease" signs.

When I asked Skip to send me a bio on his qualifications, he immediately faxed me two single spaced pages of honors, awards and accomplishments. It took me five minutes to read them all and another five minutes to get over my deep sense of inadequacy. Of all of them, however, I know he is most proud of his commitment to Big Brothers, a mentorship program that provides personal one-on-one interaction with children who can greatly benefit from added guidance.

Here is Skip's story:

"One day I located a buyer who made an acceptable offer for 17 acres of land that were part of a larger 117-acre site owned by my father and Don Kelley for 18 years. One condition of the contract was that Bob and Don would extend the road they had built on the property through the 17 acres in back."

"The buyer kept calling to remind me that the extension of the road was to be at the seller's expense. He would always end the conversation by saying that the seller would have to tear down the house to extend the road. No matter how many times I explained to him that there were no buildings on the land, he would insist that there was a house on the property. Finally, it occurred to me that he must have been looking at the wrong piece of land, and that he had negotiated a contract for the wrong site. I suggested that he and I meet at the site so he could point out the so-called house that was causing him concern."

"We met the next day, walked along various paths through the property and the buyer pointed to a house…located on the seller's property! Inside the house was a family who had been living there for 18 years!"

"No one could believe it. The title company had no record of any building improvements being located on the property, and Bob and Don had no idea anyone lived on the property. Apparently, this is what happened: When Bob and Don purchased the property, the seller met with the family living in the house to inform them that he had sold the house along with the 117 acres. Then he told the residents that, as far as he was concerned, they could stay in the house until someone asked them to leave. And it wasn't until after 18 years of free rent that anyone asked them to leave!"

If another three years had passed, the residents of the house might have contended for ownership through adverse possession. But they agreed to leave. The road was extended and Skip called his sign company to order another "Sold" sign. Lucky sign guy!

Filed Under "That's Incredible!"

THE THIRD GENTLEMAN

Dave Fox continues to win numerous design awards from The National Association of Remodeling Industry as one of the premier home remodelers in Columbus, and has been named one of the "Big 50" in the U.S. by Remodeling Magazine. Dave, however, is most proud of the Business Integrity Award he received from the Better Business Bureau.

Dave was 30 years old when he got a call from his friend, Bob, who asked Dave to meet him at a vacant landsite located on Henderson Road. Bob was considering buying the land and building a restaurant. Dave met him at the site and was introduced to another gentleman, dressed rather plainly in a pair of khakis and a cotton shirt.

The three of them discussed the size of the ground and the value of the site from the standpoint of putting up a restaurant. Neither Dave nor Bob had any real experience in owning a restaurant, so the third gentleman, who had recently opened up his first restaurant downtown was the "expert" of the group.

Dave Fox said he would build the restaurant if his friend Bob decided to go ahead and make the land purchase. Dave listened politely to the third gentleman who suggested that since Dave was a builder, maybe he should build on the site, and if all things went well, he could even build another restaurant for himself. Dave didn't know anything about operating a restaurant, but the gentleman insisted that he could supply the expertise for a "fee," so to speak. Dave was told that for a fee of $10,000, he would be taught everything from preparing the meals to hiring the employees.

Dave Fox explains it this way. "You could tell that he was really a very nice man. But I just couldn't get over the idea that he wanted me to give him $10,000 to teach me how to flip burgers!"

Dave politely declined the offer. The other Dave, R. David Thomas, returned to his restaurant downtown on East Broad Street, to the restaurant he named after one of his daughters, Wendy.

Dave Thomas went on to open up, oh, a few more restaurants. Dave Fox sometimes wonders what might have happened had he decided to build the burger shop, which would have been the first spin-off of one of the most successful fast food enterprises in history. But as I told Dave, in retrospect, it would seem kind of nutty for a 30-year-old making a good start in the construction business to drop what he's doing and start learning burgers and fries. None of us owns a crystal ball.

The reason I enjoy hearing that story is because Dave tells of the missed opportunity with humor. I am sure that this same great attitude is the reason Dave Fox Remodeling has become such a tremendous success and continues to be recognized both locally and regionally. We should all be so fortunate!

Filed Under "That's Incredible!"

I HAPPENED TO READ AN ARTICLE IN THE PAPER

Perhaps you have seen Curt Arnspiger at Midwest air shows flying his vintage airplane in various circles, climbs, spins, and dives. Curt is an avid pilot who has flown around the world.

Curt began his investment in real estate by purchasing doubles and four-family apartment buildings. He often purchased real estate by borrowing his down payment funds from the seller, who, in turn, would secure the loan with a second mortgage on the property. Because he always borrowed so heavily against the property, his monthly debt service to the lender was higher than normal. However, Curt always generated positive cash flow by managing the property himself. If an apartment needed painting or cleaning, Curt did the work himself. If a hot water tank needed replacement, he did the replacing. After a few years, Curt sold his properties that were scattered about and bought larger numbers of apartments that were more centrally located. Within a few years, Curt owned over 150 apartments.

Then one day, he happened to read an interesting article in the newspaper.

According to the article, the lending institution that held the note and mortgage on one of Curt's properties was having all of its loans liquidated, under the direction of the Resolution Trust Corporation. Curt understood this to mean that his note was going to be sold, at a discounted price, to the highest bidding bank. Curt wondered if he could enter the bidding process. The worst thing they could do was simply say "no", which was exactly what he expected them to do.

Imagine Curt's surprise when they responded with an offer to discount his loan by 15% if he prepaid his loan! Immediately, Curt contacted another lender who agreed to refinance Curt's discounted loan amount and even offered to lower his interest rate!

According to Curt, his good fortune was the result of not one, but two things. "First, I was at the right place at the right time. Second, but just as important, I had to *know* that I was in the right place at the right time. If I hadn't read that article in the paper, it would have just been a lost opportunity."

Filed Under "That's Incredible!"

HE REALLY INVESTED HIS MONEY IN LAND

Whenever Jean Snyder is coordinating a closing, I know I am in good hands. The working life of a title insurance officer is extremely stressful, because any delay, problem or dispute associated with a closing usually lands on their desk first. Through it all, Jean maintains her professionalism and her great sense of humor.

And a sense of humor is what she needed the day a buyer showed up for a closing with $25,000 of tightly rolled up bundles of cash, caked with semi-dried mud, mold and bugs. Downpayment money.

"It was obvious he had buried the money for a long, long time," Jean laughs.

Well, we've always told people that if they want their money to grow, they ought to put it into real estate.

YOU'RE LOOKING AT A MILLION DOLLAR PRODUCER

It all started when Dee Amsler crashed her car into her mother's car.

Dee, her husband Bob, and their three girls had just moved from Pittsburgh and were new to Columbus. When Bob came home from work one day, Dee said, "Bob, I have good news and bad news. The bad news is I backed into Mom's car and banged up her fender."

"What's the good news?" Bob asked anxiously.

"The good news is I have enough money in my checking account to pay for the damage, so we don't have to go to the insurance company."

"What checking account?" he said. She replied, "My checking account."

"The place you put my money, that I work for, to pay the bills? That account?" he asked.

Dee blurted out, "Well, I am going to get a job. What do you think about that?"

"Sure you are. What are you going to do, Dee?" he asked.

Dee had absolutely no idea, but had to give some sort of

Filed Under "That's Incredible!"

answer. Suddenly she remembered a conversation she had with a real estate agent at a recent party. "You ought to sell real estate," the agent had told her. Dee said to Bob, "I'm going to sell real estate!"

"Oh really?" Bob said. "Who is going to hire someone with no experience?"

The agent was with HER Realtors, so she replied, "HER Realtors, that's who!"

Dee laughed when she told me the story and said, "Garry, you have to understand, when Bob and I have a disagreement, it's over in two minutes and we both forget about it forever. So I had forgotten the whole thing, until Bob came home and asked me if I had a job. And the next day he asked me again if I had a job! Each time I told him I would have a job soon!"

Dee's first interview was with Paul Bean with HER Realtors. After listening to Paul talk at length about the great people and opportunity at his company, Dee said she would like to take the job and begin working as soon as possible. Because Dee had no work experience and was completely new to Columbus, Paul explained the company policy of only hiring salespeople with experience. Dee asked what he was looking for in an agent.

"We are looking for people with experience who are million dollar producers every year," he said.

Having no idea what a million dollar producer was, Dee said, "Well, you are looking at a million dollar producer right here. And you are not going to be very happy one year from now if I am a million dollar producer with another company. I will not come work for you then, if you do not give me a chance now."

"Mrs. Amsler, you need to understand that I only recommend potential salespeople to our president, who makes the final decision." Paul said.

"Well then, do me a favor and call the president and tell him I would like to talk with him. Maybe he will realize that I am a million dollar producer!" she replied.

Walking and Talking

Paul made the call, and George Smith agreed to meet Dee the following afternoon at two o'clock.

That evening Bob asked, "Well, did you get the job?"

"Not yet," Dee said, "But I will tomorrow. I am meeting with the president of the company."

The next day, kindergarten was out at noon, and Dee's babysitter got the flu. A stressful situation for Dee. She bought candy and pop, coloring books and crayons for her daughter, Jennifer. She gave Jennifer instructions to stay in the car and to come inside if she needed her. (As Dee recounts this story, she can hardly believe the story herself!)

"Do you realize that you are looking at a million dollar producer and just do not know it yet?" Dee now asked George Smith. The interview had gone much the same way as the first one with Paul, except for one very disconcerting difference. Over George's shoulder Dee could see Jennifer in the car through the window behind George. "Oh my gosh!" she thought, "I have to hurry and get this done!" She just had to leave with a job or she would never live it down with Bob.

"Mrs. Amsler, I will agree to this if you take the necessary classes and pass the exam. Then you and I will talk again and I will consider hiring you," George said.

Dee did not even know there were classes and exams that had to be taken. Dee said that she would take the classes and pass the exam, but insisted, "You must agree now to hire me on the condition that I pass!"

Finally, George asked, "Mrs. Amsler, why is it so important you get a final answer today?"

Dee replied, "Mr. Smith, I have listened to all of my husband's sales training tapes that his company has produced. The main theme is to never, ever leave without a commitment. I need this job, and you have to give me your commitment!"

"You have my promise," he said. "You pass the exam and you can work here."

Dee handed a notepad and pen to George and asked for

him to sign a note that he would hire her.

"Why do you need that in writing, Mrs. Amsler?" he asked.

"Because I am concerned that after I have taken the classes and passed the exam, you will forget about me," she replied.

Just then, Dee saw Jennifer get out of the car, walk over to the window and look in at her.

George Smith stood up and said ,"Mrs. Dee Amsler, today is April 15th, 1976, and I guarantee you I will never forget this conversation for as long as I live!"

Today, Bob attests to the fact that Dee literally spent ten hours a day for weeks studying for that exam. When she passed her exam, Bob said, "Dee, I bet you won't last six weeks in that business."

"Well, let me explain something to you," she said. "I will last a long time, and against your masters degree and engineering education, I will make more money than you!"

"The day that happens is the day I quit my job and go into real estate myself!" Bob replied.

After Dee passed the exam, she asked if she could work the phones the following day, Labor Day, even though the office was closed. She worked Thanksgiving and New Year's Day, figuring if a potential customer called, they would work with her because she would be the only agent in the office. This was the same reason she came in at seven o'clock each morning to catch any calls that came in before the secretary arrived at 8:30. Dee also asked everyone in the office for referrals of names of any people they didn't want to work with, because the chance of making a deal was low, or the commission too small. One agent actually pulled a couple of leads out of his trashcan for her to work on.

In her first four months, Dee earned only $2,200. But by the end of the year, she had sold over 50 homes and made the Million Dollar Club.

Three years later, Dee attended the National Association of Realtors® Convention in New Orleans. Of the 450 agents with

Walking and Talking

HER Realtors®, Dee ranked #7 in sales volume. While waiting in the hotel lounge for their rooms to be ready, Dee and some of her co-workers struck up a conversation with another group of real estate agents from Texas.

When Dee mentioned she was with HER Realtors®, one of the women from Texas said, "I know HER. Harley E. Rouda spoke to our entire sales force last year. I have to ask you something that we all wanted to know after his talk. Was there really a housewife with no sales experience, from out of town, who is now one of the top agents with your company?" Dee's friends pointed at Dee and said, "It's her! It's her!"

The following year, Dee was #2 with the company. In 1982, when interest rates were 17%, Dee knew in December that she would be competing neck and neck for the #1 spot. On December 14th, Dee put a home that was under construction in-contract. It was scheduled to be completed January 7th. Dee told the builder and her buyers, "You don't understand, this deal *has* to close this year!" The builder told Dee that it just wasn't possible. "Oh, really?" They obviously underestimated Dee.

Two weeks later, Bob Amsler came home to a feast of a meal prepared by Dee and their three daughters. At his plate, sat a sheet of paper, cut up into 20 pieces. When Bob put the puzzle together, it read, "Now is a good time to eat your words and quit your job. Today I am #1."

True to his word, Bob quit his job, joined HER Realtors® and within three years, became sales manager for the Muirfield/Powell office. Bob and Dee are two of the nicest people you will ever meet. As they recounted their story, I could easily see the admiration and respect they have for each other. This leads me to Bob's story.

Filed Under "That's Incredible!"

WHAT ABOUT BOB?

"Bob! You do not understand. He will only need the car for six weeks, until he closes on his house, and he only needs to use the car to drive to and from work!" Dee Amsler said.

This was supposed to make Bob Amsler feel better about the fact that, to sell a house, his wife Dee had agreed to lend the buyer her car for the six weeks until the house closed. The buyer needed a car immediately for work, but buying it right now would throw off the financial ratios required by the bank to approve him for a house loan.

Every weekend Dee had to borrow Bob's car to show houses, deliver contracts, etc. After four weeks, Bob was extremely frustrated at being stuck at home without a car.

Then the doorbell rang.

Bob opened the door and the buyer introduced himself. In the driveway was the car, packed full of family members and boxes. Strapped to the roof of the car were pieces of furniture. It was raining. Bob was fuming.

"Could you please fix the windshield wipers to this car?" the buyer asked impatiently. "My family and I are traveling to

Chicago to visit relatives, and I cannot see a thing through the windshield in this rain."

Readers who might have criticized Bob's lack of support for Dee's early venture into sales must now grant Bob special dispensation for keeping his temper in check, fixing the wipers for the family, and wishing them a safe trip.

Not enough? How about the time Dee sold a house in less than a week, when the seller expected that it would take months to sell. The seller suggested he and his wife reject the contract because they couldn't move fast enough to accommodate the buyers. Dee said, "No problem. You can store all your house furnishings in our home, and then rent until we find you a house!"

It might have been a good idea to let Bob know about that little arrangement. Instead, Bob got out of the shower one morning and heard a commotion. He looked out the window and saw people unloading a moving van full of furniture into the door of their walkout basement.

The furniture was still there when Bob and Dee threw a holiday party for 100 guests at their home. As people began arriving, cabbage got caught in the disposal. The water was backed up for several minutes before anyone noticed. It poured through the floor onto the furniture in the basement!

Dee flew through the house with paper towels and sheets to cover the buyer's furniture. She went back upstairs. Guess who was the first person she saw? The buyer, who asked, "Dee could I please go downstairs and get an electric toothbrush I have packed in one of the boxes?" Uh oh.

How about the time Bob and Dee were shopping for a brand new refrigerator, when finally Bob said, "Dee, let's get out of here. We cannot justify buying another refrigerator right now, when ours works perfectly fine." To which Dee responded, "Bob, I hate to tell you this, but in two days one of my buyers is taking

Filed Under "That's Incredible!"

our refrigerator. The sellers just wouldn't include it in their price!"

Promoting their business became a family affair. Bob recalls how they would dress their daughter Molly in a clown outfit and sponsor various neighborhood birthday parties, graduations, and anniversaries. Molly would play a song on the boom box she carried with her that started out, "My name is Zoom and I came from the moon...." They would deliver invitations, pay for prizes, hats, and party favors. Bob was in charge of the helium balloons. Everyone helped grow the family business.

Their business continued to grow and grow. Today, Molly has joined their sales team and is celebrating her ninth year in real estate sales. Now, you have heard from the perspective of a husband, father, and real estate sales agent. That's Bob!

Walking and Talking

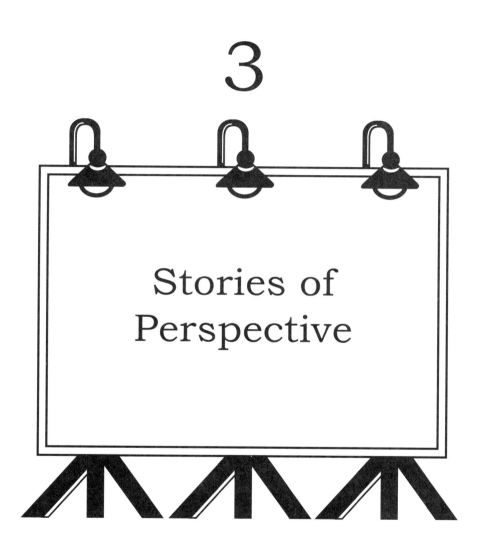

3

Stories of Perspective

Walking and Talking

Stories of Perspective

"I have always wondered at this American marvel, the great energy of the human soul that drives people to better themselves and improve the fortunes of their families and their communities. Indeed, I know of no greater force on earth."

Ronald Reagan

Stories of Perspective perfectly illustrates the one thing all of the contributors of this book have in common. Attitude! They share an optimistic perspective towards life.

They are people like Don Ray, a real estate investor who takes a positive and hopeful attitude to what the future will bring. Don's education began on a farm in Tennessee. It was there that he and his five brothers farmed 180 acres with the bare essentials of farm equipment.

Don recalls, "We had no electricity, little running water, and few tools. We plowed the fields by mule. It was very difficult work, for sure. Looking back, my father probably thought that the hard, long days of labor would keep me and my brothers out of trouble. And he was probably right."

"But as 'country' as this might sound, I really formed a concept of investment on that farm," says Don. "We planted corn, watermelon and tomatoes. Basically, we tried a little bit of everything. And I discovered you really do reap what you sow. Some plantings die off completely, some have average results, and others do great! I learned that you cannot expect a 100% harvest of everything you sow. But more importantly, I learned that if you do not sow anything, you do not have any chance at all of a harvest. That is how I always viewed the businesses I started and the real estate properties I purchased."

"They will not all grow to your expectations, but some of them will do fine and others will pleasantly surprise you. But nothing will mature and ripen if you do not plant any seeds at all. The more seeds you plant along the way, the greater your opportunity is for a bountiful harvest."

Like Don, the contributors to *Walking and Talking* like to plant seeds and watch things grow. Here are some of their stories…

Stories of Perspective

KEEPING PERSPECTIVE

A couple of years ago, I spent the afternoon trying to make the most of my midlife crisis by mountain biking down a steep, wet, slippery hill, laden with rocks and tree roots. It was at that moment that I went airborne. It is a very odd feeling because it happens so fast and there is little you can do except wait and see what part of you breaks. Will you land on a tree stump? Or a rock? I landed on my shoulder. One of my biking partners that day, Sidney Noblitt, drove me to the hospital, while the other, Jack Baruth, tended to what they both considered to be the more important job: fixing my bike.

Dr. Michael McShane just shook his head at me when he looked at the x-rays. Mike is a good friend of mine who also happens to be an outstanding orthopedic surgeon. I asked the obligatory question of how long it would take before I would be shooting golf in the 70's. When he estimated it would take between two and three months, I told him how happy I was because it had been years since I had broken 90. Mike is used to my bad jokes.

One Sunday morning at church, my family and I happened

to be standing next to Mike and his wife Kim, when all of a sudden, their daughter came running up the aisle.

"Dad, come quick! Somebody just fainted and had a bad fall!" she said.

As Mike followed her to give his medical attention, I looked at Kim and said, "You are not going to believe this, but the exact same thing happened to me last week."

"Really?" she replied.

"Same thing," I said. "Michelle came running up the aisle, looked at me and said, 'Come quick... somebody wants to make an offer on a four-family building!'"

The point here is not just that I go around all day telling goofy jokes to people, but that sometimes we need to take a step back and give proper perspective to our careers. I do not want to underestimate the importance of giving good investment advice to people who rely on us to give them solid recommendations that will affect their retirement and financial independence. But we are not doing surgery, fighting crime, putting out house fires, giving aid to the sick, helping to save souls or standing ready to protect the American way of life. That is left to doctors, police officers, firefighters, nurses, clergy and soldiers.

When we get caught up putting together that next big deal, it is easy to lose perspective and forget that all we are really doing is giving advice. Of course, good advice can be a great thing. For instance, Jack gave me great advice right before I went airborne, when he said, "If you're not sure about that hill, today's not the day to try." That was advice I should have taken!

Stories of Perspective

A GREAT START TO THE DAY

The line of cars turning into the convention center's parking garage was backed up over a block and moving excruciatingly slow. Up ahead I saw an open space on the street with a parking meter and decided it was my best bet for being on time for my breakfast meeting. I fumbled for change from the ashtray and put a quarter in the meter. That bought me about eight minutes. Instead of asking the gentleman walking past me on the sidewalk if he could spare 43 quarters, I resigned myself to getting a ticket and left to meet my friend.

I had been graciously invited to attend the annual Ohio Prayer Breakfast, where the speakers would include Ohio Governor Bob Taft, Ohio Secretary of State J. Kenneth Blackwell and retired coach of the 1990 National Champion University of Colorado football team, Bill McCartney.

As I walked in the huge hall reserved for the early morning event, I was struck by the large number of people who were in attendance. Well over a thousand people from all walks of life were there. People from the world of business, politics, education, government, church and media were all represented. I saw several people I hadn't seen for a while and ran into a friend of mine from college, Chip Weiant.

Chip Weiant is founder and principal of CompassUSA, a company that works one-on-one with leaders of companies to accurately assess their company, from the very foundation on up, to rebuild and strengthen character-based relationships throughout their organization. Replacing the weaker "knowledge-based" management perspective with the more powerful "character-based" leadership perspective creates the kind of culture in which tangible and positive improvements can be made to the strategies, systems and structure of a company. Whew! One day I finally had to ask Chip what that all meant!

"Okay Scan. Let me explain it this way. Whenever world class athletes are asked to discuss the reasons for their success, they always talk about character aspects: perseverance, discipline, sacrifice, effort, passion, etc. They talk about their belief system. They do not talk about their skill levels, their competencies, their knowledge. They talk about what they believe in; what they are!" Chip says. "That is because character has its foundation in deep-seated beliefs and truths, and beliefs and truths will trump competencies or raw knowledge every time."

Chip believes that companies, unfortunately, tend to focus heavily on the knowledge-based management training approach. They err towards increasing knowledge because it is easily quantified. The thought is, all I need to do is take more classes and I will get an MBA and I will succeed. The manager sets up a certain amount of classes and training for the employees to increase their knowledge in expectation they will reach greater achievement. While this approach might be helpful, it is extremely limited.

Real leadership, however, involves integrating a belief system that is character-based. According to Chip, "You do not learn how to *do* respect. You must *be* respectful. You do not learn how to *do* honesty or *do* compassion. You must *be* honest and *be* compassionate. A company is really just a big team. If that team shares a vocabulary and a commitment towards building character-based relationships throughout each department of the company, they become unbeatable!"

Chip feels so strongly that leaders, in particular, need to be outfitted with a defined character ethic code, that he authored a 20-point creed called "Uncommon Sense", which was adopted by the Secretary of State as a model for Ohio's business and government leaders.

The talk around the tables and throughout the room that morning was not about the "deals" everyone was doing, or the different projects they were working on; but instead, the conversation was focused on relationships and family activities, between people who genuinely wanted to better know one another. That is amazing, considering the wide variety of people in attendance that day.

If what 20th century writer George Bernanos said is true, that "The wish for prayer is a prayer in itself," then I hope the Ohio Prayer Breakfast continues to meet for years to come on the first Thursday of May, in observance of the National Day of Prayer, declared by Congress in 1952 and amended and signed in 1988 by President Ronald Reagan.

When it was over, I got in my car in a great mood, ready to take on the day. I had eaten delicious food, listened to motivating speeches and enjoyed wonderful company. What could be better? Well, not finding that bright orange parking ticket on my windshield could be better.

LEARNING TO TEACH
(OR TEACHING TO LEARN)

One of the greatest experiences I have enjoyed in recent years is to help conduct a series of economic classes for the 8th grade class at Saint Andrew Grade School. Junior Achievement of America recruits individuals from the business world to discuss with students such topics as how to balance a check book, interview for a job, buy a house, invest in the stock market, etc. I have been given tremendous support and encouragement by Mary Beth Day, a wonderful teacher who has earned numerous teaching awards, and Michael Scurria, Junior Achievement's Middle School Teacher of the Year 2001 in Columbus, Ohio. For 10 years he has taken time out of his business schedule to help instruct young people as they prepare for high school.

One day, to begin a discussion on the topic of wages, I asked the class, "I like that doctors earn a good income. Can anyone think of a reason why it might be a good thing that doctors earn a good income?" The first person to raise their hand said, "Because it gives them motivation to study hard and attend extra years at medical school."

Stories of Perspective

The next student answered, "Because our health is one of the most important things we have."

Another student said, "I know why you do! So you can sell them real estate!"

Everyone seemed to be getting a kick out of that response when suddenly an arm shot up and began waving wildly back and forth. "Oh oh oh, I know, I know!" The student was so excited, he could hardly contain himself.

"Yes," I said. "Why do you think it might be a good thing that doctors earn a good living?"

"Because my Dad's a doctor!" he replied.

We have a lot of laughs and learn a lot from each other. One thing I try to impress on the kids is that most of us develop patterns of behavior, at a very young age, that impact our chances for future success and happiness. Even the young eighth-graders continually make decisions that will play a major role in determining how they will spend their adult life. Hopefully, they will consider this as they begin to make choices regarding alcohol, drugs, physical fitness, friends, mentors, work ethics, etc.

We discuss how important it is to be honest, work hard, follow your dreams, don't worry about failures, don't worry about always fitting in with the crowd, have confidence in yourself, understand the importance of your friends and family, etc. The positive impact on both the kids and the instructors is tremendous.

You end up learning a great deal more than you teach, when you volunteer your time to Junior Achievement.

Walking and Talking

IF YOU ARE GOING TO DO NOTHING...DO NOTHING WELL

One of the hardest working agents in our office came into my office one day with a depressed look on his face.

"It seems like everyone I call is either out of the office, in a meeting or on vacation. My closing on the office building is being delayed until next week, and my two o'clock appointment cancelled because he's sick. It's hard to stay motivated when nobody seems to want to work!" he said.

His expression told me he was looking for some inspiration. Maybe an idea of how he could kick-start his day and make it productive. I told him to get out of the office!

"Get out of here," I told him. "Look, today just doesn't seem to be happening for you. No one is around. Obviously, you are not in the best of moods. It's a beautiful day. Take the afternoon off. Go hit 18! Tomorrow's another day."

Every once in a while, if you are going to do nothing, then do nothing well! Recharge the batteries. Relax and play golf. Ride a bike or play tennis. Do anything that will take your mind off work so that you can return the next day and be extra pro-

Stories of Perspective

ductive. In this case, the agent was very hard working, needed a break and decided to hit golf balls at the driving range. He returned the next day with renewed energy and an improved attitude. People were more available and he was hitting on all cylinders again.

Hanging around the office, trying to 'force the action' is not always the best plan of attack. If you are doing nothing anyway, do nothing well and have some fun.

CHEESE PIES

George Bakallis grew up in, Athens, Greece. He remembers the countless hours he spent as a child playing soccer not too far from the Acropolis. At the very young age of 10, George made a decision that dramatically impacted his life. More about that later...

George arrived in America with a student visa in 1964. After graduating from college, George obtained a masters degree in engineering at Ohio University. George began work as a quality control engineer for a car parts manufacturer. There he was granted a lunch break every day, with evenings and weekends off. George made good use of that time.

In 1973 George purchased his first rental property. Over the next seven years he accumulated additional real estate. George filled those lunch breaks, evenings and weekends making repairs, painting and cleaning. His free time was spent leasing apartments, paying bills and locating more real estate. After seven years, George decided to quit his full time job and devote all of his attention to real estate investment.

While there was still plenty to do, George considers this a

time of "semi-retirement", because although he was working, he was making his own schedule and enjoyed what he was doing. It certainly did not feel like a job.

At this point, George strayed from the strategy of most investors. Instead of seeking to acquire additional real estate, George determined that once he paid off the loans on the real estate he already owned, the property would generate enough cash flow for him to happily retire. Instead of buying more and more real estate, George targeted his energy towards paying off the loans on his existing rental property.

Every investor should do this. If your goal is to own real estate as a vehicle to retirement, determine how much annual income you need when you retire. For example, if you desire to retire with an annual income of $100,000 per year, then you should purchase $1,000,000 of real estate that generates a 10% return once the loan is paid off. Then, work towards paying off the loan to reach your retirement goal.

It is surprising how rare it is for real estate investors to take this approach. Instead of asking themselves how much cash flow is enough for them to meet their financial goals, they become fixated on the notion that the more real estate they own, the more equity they will create, ultimately resulting in even more cash flow. While this might be true, the word "ultimately" needs to be considered. Typically, the more real estate an investor purchases and the higher the debt leverage becomes, the longer it takes to pay off the property. The possibility for higher reward is greater, but so too is the risk.

I met George several years ago when he exchanged his original properties for newer, professionally managed apartments. While we have become good friends, he does not let that get in the way of beating me in racquetball or missing an opportunity to tell me that I work too hard. "Slow down." he says. "Take time to enjoy life." George is one who lives what he preaches. His advice is to determine how much income is necessary to maintain your personal lifestyle, and target that as your goal.

At the young age of ten, George made a life-changing decision to become economically disciplined. He vowed to spend no more than one-tenth of the amount of money he had in his wallet. He still remembers how challenging it was for him to resist the delicious cheese pies that the baker down the street sold for 1 drachma. "But, if I only had 8 drachmas in my wallet, I would not buy the pie. I would wait until I saved up 2 more drachmas." George recalls, "I saw that my parents were big spenders, which is understandable given all the wonderful things there are to do in Greece - the travel, the entertainment, the food. But, somehow that made me even more determined to limit my spending to one-tenth of what I had in my wallet. I later expanded that strategy to include larger items. For instance, I would never buy a car that costs more than one-tenth of the savings I have in the bank. The only exception to this rule is real estate, which is a commodity that appreciates, rather than depreciates in value."

George's strategy enabled him to retire before the age of forty. Today, he resides in his native Greece, enjoying the climate, the water, and an occassional cheese pie.

Stories of Perspective

PLANTING FLOWERS

Owning investment real estate is a great way to control a large asset that will eventually be paid off, free of all debt, generating profit. As with anything, there is certainly some risk involved, but all aspects of life involve risk. What is the downside to all of this? Property management.

What a difficult thing it is to effectively manage investment real estate. If you are a property manager, you can relate to the frequent incoming calls all day long from people with problems and complaints. A disposal is plugged up, or the air conditioning is not working, etc., etc. Fortunately, there are professional managers who are temperamentally suited for the job. One such person is Jim Cunningham with CASTO. Jim manages thousands of apartments and scores of retail shopping centers for owners who want the benefits of owning real estate without the hassles of management.

Others decide to both own and manage their real estate. Such a person is H. Roger Neal. Twenty-five years ago, Roger was working for the city repairing underground sewers. Looking for a change, Roger set out to buy very inexpensive single-family homes and dilapidated doubles, make any needed repairs, and lease them in good condition to qualified residents. Today, Roger Neal owns and manages several hundred apartments.

One of Roger's most rewarding experiences involved the purchase of a small single family home that was in complete disrepair. Roger replaced the roof, the carpeting and the appliances. He installed a new HVAC system and updated the electric. He repaired windows, hauled away junk and landscaped the yard.

He then sold the home, that for years had been used as a rental property, to a lady in the neighborhood who made it her home.

"Don't get me wrong," Roger says. "I made a profit for my effort. But it was great to see the smile on her face when she bought the only home she had ever owned. I closed that house three years ago. I guarantee you, if you drive by that house right now, it will be the best-landscaped yard in the neighborhood. She planted one hundred flowers and keeps her home beautiful."

The most rewarding property management of all!

Stories of Perspective

LOOK WHAT THE WIND BLEW IN!

Sitting alone at a round table with place settings for eight, I watched as dozens, and then hundreds, of people began pouring through the doors of the convention center to attend the annual awards luncheon hosted by The Better Business Bureau of Columbus. Some friends of mine, from our days at Miami University, had mentioned earlier in the week that one of our fellow classmates, and former college roommate of mine, Bill Owens, was to be awarded the 2001 Integrity Award for Central Ohio. Waiting for my friends to arrive, I read the BBB's literature about Bill Owens, which began by citing his BA in Philosophy. Philosophy? An odd major for someone who could take some wood and build anything, and who would go on to found Owens Construction Company two years after graduation. Philosophy! How could I have forgotten that? But there was one thing about Bill I will never forget. It has to do with Hurricane Andrew.

It has been over ten years since that disaster blew into South Florida at wind speeds approaching 175 miles per hour, yet if you log onto the internet today and type in "Hurricane Andrew," you will get over 73,000 hits. The destruction in Homestead,

Walking and Talking

Florida extended for miles. Homes were obliterated, telephone poles were cut in half and neighborhoods were flooded. No gas, electric or water service was available. In less than a few hours, on August 24th, 1992, Andrew had caused damage estimated at 30 billion dollars. Thirty thousand million dollars! More importantly, hundreds of thousands of residents were left homeless. Not the place to be, I thought. Apparently Bill thought differently.

"What's new Bets?" I asked Bill's wife, Betsy, a real estate agent.

"Not much Scan. I just got back from Homestead," she said.

"Homestead? What in the world were you doing down there?" I asked.

Betsy explained that Bill decided to spend a few weeks in Homestead in the aftermath of the hurricane, and that she had gone down with their baby son to add support. "You cannot believe the devastation down there. All of the road signs are gone, so it was almost impossible to find Bill!"

The idea of the two of them, and their new son, traveling to Homestead at a time when their business was still growing was hard to understand. Maybe Bill was taking advantage of some great work opportunities.

"He is getting paid well, I hope," I said to Betsy.

Betsy laughed, "No, Scan. He's not getting paid. It's just something he wants to do. He heard that people needed help, so he threw his tools in the truck and drove south!"

What a neat feeling it was to be there at the luncheon, almost 10 years later, reading about Bill's years of positive influence in the field of construction, his participation on task forces, trade organizations and community service projects and his company's success and commitment to volunteer work. In September of 2005 Hurricane Katrina's impact on New Orleans reminded us once again that weather disasters will always occur from time to time. It is good to know that people like Bill and Betsy Owens will always respond.

4

A Very Special Person

Walking and Talking

A Very Special Person

NICOLE MOORE WILCOX

I can be overly impulsive sometimes. That is why, after placing an advertisement in the paper for a sales assistant, I promised myself to interview at least eight people who responded to the ad. My plan included holding a second round of interviews with the four best candidates before narrowing the choice down to two people who I would interview for a third time. Only then would I make a final decision. This was an extremely important position to fill. I prepared myself with a long list of open and closed-ended questions for the interviews. I was ready!

My first interview was with a young lady by the name of Nicole Moore. Thirty minutes later, I was elated when she accepted the position!

Nicole was articulate, friendly and confident. You could immediately sense that she was very honest, energetic and talented. I remember thinking if Nicole ended up being only half as good as she appeared, she would be outstanding. Actually, she was over-qualified for the position. It was not long before she had greatly improved the entire structure of the office. She

Walking and Talking

was organized and creative, and she took it upon herself to think of ways to continually expand my business.

Her great sense of humor and her genuine interest in other people made her an instant favorite of everyone in the office. A natural born teacher, Nicole was always willing to help anyone who asked her for advice and opinions on computers, marketing and advertising, and sometimes, even on things relating to their personal lives. She became a close friend to all of us.

In a short time, she was meeting directly with investors, appraisers, title company representatives, lenders and attorneys. I used to joke that everyone enjoyed working with Nicole more than with me, until I noticed that instead of laughing, they would look at me with an expression that said, "Yeah, you are right, so what's your point, Garry?"

We learned never to be surprised at what Nicole could do. Her memory for numbers became legendary. She remembered any phone number or any address she heard. If Nicole was asked the telephone number or address of a person who had called in one time, six months earlier, she would not even have to look the number up on the computer or in the phone book. She could rattle it off the top of her head. I once asked Nicole if she played a musical instrument. I was not the least bit surprised when she said, "Actually, my mother taught me to read music before I even learned to read. I remember being very surprised when one of my friends in third grade told me she couldn't read music. I just thought everyone knew how to read music, just like everyone knew how to read English."

Six months later, Nicole married Randy Wilcox, and you just knew it was a match made in heaven. A year later, Nicole announced the great news that they were expecting their first child, a baby girl. It was wonderful to see how well Nicole was balancing all of the new things in her life.

Two months before their daughter Riley was born, Nicole

was diagnosed with breast cancer. Her reaction was not one of concern for herself, but instead, for the health of her unborn child. She delayed the treatment of her illness so the baby could more fully develop. Nicole was tremendously thankful and relieved when Riley was born without any complications.

Over the next several months, Nicole endured countless sessions of chemotherapy and radiation treatments. She shortened her schedule at work to spend more time with Riley and to fight the brutal side effects of the treatments.

The courage Nicole showed during this time in her life is indescribable. I remember feeling angry when someone mentioned that it almost appeared as if Nicole was in denial regarding her physical condition. How else could you explain her extremely upbeat and positive attitude? Those close to Nicole, however, knew that within two weeks of her diagnosis, she had researched and learned more about breast cancer than had many doctors. She scoured the internet, read books on the subject, joined support groups and consulted various doctors. Denial was not part of Nicole's makeup. But, given the positive way in which she chose to react to her condition, it is easy to understand why others were in awe and wonder.

During this fight for her life, Nicole never lost her great sense of humor or her interest in other people. She organized a Race for The Cure Golf Outing to raise funds for research. And never, never once, did I hear Nicole utter a single word of complaint.

One day after work, I visited Nicole at the hospital. With Randy next to her, Nicole calmly told me that they had met a couple of hours earlier with their doctor who had explained that all treatments had been exhausted, and they should make arrangements for hospice care. A few minutes later, a nurse came in with dinner for Nicole. I felt like I should leave, but Nicole asked that I stay and visit while Randy got something to eat at the cafeteria.

Nicole asked if my step-daughter, Michelle, had decided where to go to college, and gave suggestions of places she might want to consider. She asked how everyone was doing at the office. She talked about how fortunate it was that her daughter Riley was doing so well, and told me how badly she felt for Randy. The only thing she could not reconcile to herself was how difficult this was going to be for Randy who had been so great to her. With Nicole, it was always about other people.

Nicole's life ended in December of 2000. The tremendous impact she had on other people's lives was evident as people gathered to give their last respects. Nicole taught us about laughter, courage and priority. She reminded us that in the grand scheme of things we are all here for only a very short period of time. Through example, Nicole Moore Wilcox taught us that how well we live our life is more important than how long we live our life.

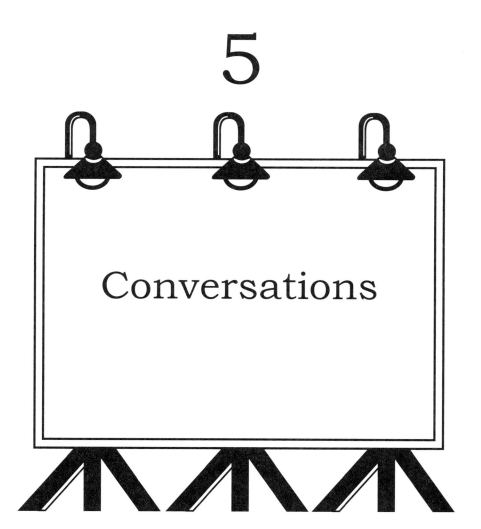

Walking and Talking

Conversations

"A single conversation across the table with a wise man is better than ten years' study of books."
Henry Wadsworth Longfellow

The most valuable currency in real estate is **Conversation**.

Conversation is where you hear about that great loan program, that available property, or that good idea that reveals a tremendous opportunity.

Following are conversations from more winners in the marketplace…

PERSISTENT "POSS" ABILITIES

Nancy Poss glanced up from the luncheon menu and, in a matter-of-fact way, said, "You know Garry, I really do not have a sales personality."

You might think this is an odd thing for Nancy to say, considering that during her career she became the #1 Re/Max agent in Central Ohio and has, on several occasions, made the list of top 100 Re/Max agents in the world. However, having sold investment property to Nancy in the past, I understood exactly what she meant.

Nancy Poss has a relaxed, easygoing bearing. With a personality that verges on nonchalance, Nancy is to real estate what Freddie Couples is to golf. She does not have that hard charging, "Type A" personality, so often associated with sales success. Yet, this part-time nurse with no sales experience moved from Aiken, South Carolina to Columbus, Ohio (where she did not know a single person), and became a top sales producer. How did she do it? That day over lunch, Nancy told me her story.

Conversations

The middle child of 10 kids, Nancy grew up in Buffalo, New York. Her father was a car mechanic who literally learned how to build houses from reading books. As Nancy recalls, "My father and my uncle spent evenings and weekends building houses. Dad was self-taught and he and Mom always stressed the importance of education. It must have worked. All ten kids ended up with scholarships to college. When my husband and I purchased a small investment property, I thought it would be a good idea to take some real estate classes."

"I will never forget when the instructor told our class of 30 students, 'One year from now, only two of you will be in real estate.' That was certainly a very sobering thought. Given the poor market conditions at the time, however, maybe the instructor was trying to be encouraging!" Nancy says.

Six months later, in 1980, the real estate company that Nancy worked for closed.

Nancy recalls her move to BuyOhio, a larger real estate company. "I was not very motivated for the first couple of years. But, I took several continuing education classes, learned some good marketing ideas, and began holding open houses for homebuilders on the weekends. Our kids and I launched a flyer campaign with the money I earned as a nurse. Gradually, the slow housing market improved, interests rates came down, and I started to get busy. Still, it was five years before I felt confident enough to give up nursing to sell real estate full-time, and in 1986 I began selling for Re/Max."

"I have a service personality," Nancy says. "I never use hard-sell techniques, but instead, I try to use a soft touch. Any success I have had has come from persistence, patience and honesty. My business just continued to slowly build. Now, seventy-five percent of my activity comes from repeat customers and referrals." (Last year Nancy's sales exceeded 40 million dollars.) "So, I formed a team with my son Keith Poss and a team of buyer agents and listing coordinators at Keller Williams Capital Partners. Having the team allows me to maintain balance between my work and personal life, yet still provide top quality service to my customers."

"Seven years ago, without even telling me, Keith took his real estate classes and announced he was going to sell. He was one of the first Realtors to design a web page. The results from that site were slow at first, but have since been outstanding. Just this week we closed a $450,000 house from that site," Nancy says. "Combining service with technology will always be key. The face-to-face meeting and the hands-on attention, however, will always be of primary importance. Keith is very good at those things."

Nancy insists she never foresaw her success. She recalls a time early in her career when she was showing houses: "One afternoon, years ago, an ice storm had left every tree branch, sidewalk and yard, covered with ice. A married couple and I skated on our shoes from tree trunks to light posts to front doors. It was so icy, we actually had to sit down and skid down the driveway! If you had told me back then that I would end up winning sales awards, I would have been skeptical. But they did buy a house that day! Garry, I would have to say, for me, it came down to persistence."

If only Nancy had a sales personality!

Conversations

IN PARTNERSHIP

I asked Stan Ackley why he decided to go into the field of real estate.

Stan replied, "After graduating from Dennison University in 1963, I made a commission on the sale of a $37,500 double. After that, do you think I would ever go back to doing anything else?" So Stan joined his uncle's firm, the Wallace F. Ackley Company.

Stan recalls a lesson he learned from his uncle. "When I first got in the business, my uncle was developing land that he had purchased, one section at a time. I asked him why he didn't just build everything at the same time. He said, 'You can eat an elephant, if you cut it up into small enough pieces.' He taught me that you need to have a lot of patience in this business."

The real estate world of business is littered with stories of partnerships that have gone awry. Even under the best of circumstances, partnerships between well-intentioned people often end up with poor results, and it is difficult to find even a handful that have worked out well. So how has Stan Ackley successfully formed twenty-three long-lasting, successful partnerships that own over three million square feet of office buildings, apartments and warehouses?

According to Stan, it all comes down to surrounding yourself with good people. "This is a personality business. Everyone likes being around a person who has a smile on their face. What would it be like to go to work every day with people you don't like? Most of the deals I do come from other real estate guys I have known for years. Choose partners that you like, and who like you. That is the most important thing."

"Partnerships are fantastic, because they allow you to diversify your ownership of real estate. And in the long run, the best way to earn money in real estate is through ownership. By partnering with other people, you diffuse the risk on any one particular transaction," Stan says. "The difficulty is handling all of the property management."

Stan continues, "Property management is a detail business. You have to get the individual parts done and then piece them all together. I like every facet of real estate, but my least favorite is certainly property management. But it is essential to success."

Over the years of managing real estate, Stan has seen some funny things. One time an apartment was being "turned" for a new resident. Carpets were shampooed, repairs were made and walls were painted. To the surprise of the cleaning person, she spotted a large snake in the apartment. She described the snake to an expert at the Columbus Zoo, who not only identified it as a python, but also explained that her sighting was actually not that unusual.

"We had to disclose to the new resident that we had seen the snake, thought it was gone, but couldn't know for sure," Stan said. "To our surprise, the new tenants had no problem occupying the apartment. He kind of looked upon it as an adventure. When his lease expired and he moved out, he joked that we misrepresented the property and he was disappointed

Conversations

that the snake never appeared."

Stan turned the tables on me when I asked him to recall his favorite purchase of property. Stan asked, "You tell me, what was your best deal?" My face went blank as I tried to answer his question. I had to admit that nothing immediately came to mind. Stan laughed, "You see? It's not the sticks and bricks you remember. It's the people."

HAVEN'T WE HAD THIS CONVERSATION ONCE BEFORE?

Every real estate transaction has its own unique set of circumstances. These circumstances can result in great opportunities, as well as tremendous challenges. Because of this, real estate can at times be exhilarating and exasperating, but never dull.

Since the world of real estate seems to change every day, it is impossible to write down rules for every situation that might occur. Therefore, precedents take on a great deal of importance. Cole Ellis told me this story regarding an interesting precedent.

"This story involves a precedent that took place my second year selling real estate. I met with an investor interested in buying a four-family building priced at $170,000. I drove the investor to the property, explained the various details of the property, provided income and expense information, and prepared a proforma of possible future performance. He wanted to take some time before making a buying decision."

"Three weeks later, another agent walked in our office with a signed contract for the same building from the same investor. I was upset, to put it mildly."

Conversations

"I approached the other agent and explained the circumstances. The other agent said he understood my frustration, but he felt that three weeks was enough time to establish that I had abandoned my efforts with the buyer. He believed a lot of time had passed and that it was his effort, not mine, that had resulted in the buyer writing a contract for the property. He did not include me in any part of the commission. This set an important precedent."

"Two years later, I located a buyer for an $8 million investment property. The sale amount and resulting commission was to be the highest I had earned since entering the field of real estate. Two days before closing, that same agent I described earlier in the story, suggested that perhaps he should share in the commission, because he claimed to have presented the same property to the same investor six months earlier. Even a referral fee on a deal this size would be a significant commission."

"I reminded the agent of his previously rendered opinion that three weeks represented 'abandonment.' Regardless of the size of the deal and the large amount of commission involved, a precedent had been set. What had gone around had come around, as we so often say in this business."

"To the other agent's credit, he agreed that my decision was consistent and fair, shook my hand, and went on to his next deal. If we ever end up working on the same real estate deal in the future, I'm sure we will work together very well."

Precedents, such as the one made in Cole's story, are made almost every day. We make decisions, some small and some large, regarding our relationships with buyers, sellers, lenders and agents all the time. The above example is by no means unusual. Precedents, understandings, working agreements, and so forth are continually created and enforced on an informal basis. Anyone in the business for the long term understands the importance of forming them with a lot of reason, thought and consideration.

THAT'S JUST NOT THE STANDARD WAY!

It was finally closing day. The apartment community we listed and placed in contract was owned by two of the nicest gentlemen in town. The property was well built and well located. However, the owners no longer believed it was an efficient use of their time to oversee the management of the property.

We had found the perfect buyer. He owned similar properties and had the ability to operate the property at maximum efficiency, allowing him to pay a strong market price. However, he was having second thoughts about being able to generate the projected cash flow. Some call this cognitive dissonance, others refer to it as buyer's remorse, but the technical term we use is "getting the heeby jeebies." His cause for concern was reasonably valid, given the uncertainty of the real estate market at that time.

So, the buyer decided to be creative. He obtained a line of credit secured by equity he had in other properties he owned so that he would have funds available in the event he had short-term cash flow problems. He also came up with another idea that he didn't share with us until the actual day of closing.

Conversations

He determined that the property would not generate cash flow if the real estate taxes were increased to reflect the new purchase price. Therefore, he decided he would only purchase the property if the sale price was reduced by 6%. To be fair to the owner, however, he would pay the 6% commission. Otherwise, he would not buy the property.

The seller's attorney did not want to make the change, because it was not the "standard" way these transactions take place. We were at a complete standstill, because the buyer felt that the real estate commission should be paid separately, by the buyer, just as the legal fees were being paid separately by the seller. I asked the attorney why he was so concerned with the change even though it did not change the net proceeds to the sellers. "Because it is never done that way," he said.

"Probably, because people haven't thought of doing it that way," I replied. "I cannot even remember the last time I actually saw a 'standard' deal. No two contracts are ever identical. Had I brought you a contract at a lower price with the buyer paying the commission, I certainly would have recommended you accept it!"

He said, "Well, that would be different, if it was in the contract." So someone suggested we just tear up the contract, return the buyer's security deposit and start all over. This met with everyone's approval and off we went to another negotiated contract and a successful closing. Good ethics and law must always be followed. However, the only real standard regarding real estate transactions is that they are standardly very different from each other.

Walking and Talking

GET OUT OF THE CAR!

It was a warm and sunny day. I jumped in my car and drove to a group of 68 apartments consisting of 34 doubles that were in various states of disrepair. They had been offered to a buyer I was representing, a developer who was considering purchasing the apartments with the idea of making substantial physical improvements to the property, such as replacing roofs, carpeting and HVAC, then selling each double individually at an increased price. He asked me to take a look at the property and give an overall opinion of how much work was required, what price we could resell the property for, and what he could expect in net proceeds from the sale.

I drove up and down the street several times, turned into all of the back parking lots, circled the neighborhood and returned back to the site. While listening to the radio, I took note of the condition of the roofs, the separately metered utilities and the various "sleeve" air conditioners in the windows. After writing down all of my notes, I was about to return to the office when suddenly I remembered some advice given to me years earlier. Get out of the car!

Conversations

Whenever I talk about getting out of the car, most people look at me like I'm nuts for even discussing something that is so obvious. "Duh, get out of the car? Thanks Garry." But it is one of those simple truths that often gets ignored.

I stepped out of the car and walked around. Over the next half hour, I talked with residents who were outside their apartments. Were they happy living here? How much is the rent? Who pays for water, gas and electric? Do the appliances work? How much are the security deposits? Any roof leaks?

I walked around backyards, tiptoeing past the "grenades" in the grass. They obviously allowed large dogs here. I made a mental note to ask about their pet policy. Looking at the soil erosion around the basement window wells caused me concern regarding possible water in the basements. The cracks in the asphalt seemed more severe when I stood on the driveways. I was certainly getting a closer look at the property. I learned things that helped my buyer make an informed decision.

The buyer purchased the apartments, spent approximately $10,000 per apartment in improvements and closing costs (both buying and selling), and profited $7,000 per apartment. A win-win situation for the residents, the investors, the contractors, the real estate agents, the title company and the buyer.

Returning to the office, I resolved to always get out of the car; rain, snow or shine, and really get a feel for the property. Simple, obvious, but critical.

DIFFERENT PERSPECTIVES

One of the best quotes I ever read was by B.C. Forbes. He said, "It is better to buy a great investment at a fair price, than a fair investment at a great price." Nowhere is this truer than with investment real estate.

In general terms, the price of investment real estate is mostly determined by the amount of net income (income less expenses) generated by the property. If a property has an annual net income of $100,000, you might expect a buyer to pay a price of one million dollars. At this price, the buyer's $100,000 annual net income represents a 10% "cash-on-cash" return on the one million dollar down payment.

Most people, however, do not have one million dollars to use as a down payment, and those who do are seldom willing to part with the entire amount. They will borrow money from a lender who will typically loan up to 80% of the purchase price, which in this example is $800,000. If a buyer borrows $800,000 at an 8.9% interest rate, amortized over 25 years, the annual loan payments total approximately $80,000 per year. So now, instead of having $100,000 in cash flow, the buyer is left with only $20,000.00. But what a great return!

Purchase Price $1,000,000
Buyer's Equity Down Payment
(20% of purchase price): .... $ 200,000
Cash Flow Return
(=Income-Expenses-Loan Payments): .... $ 20,000 (10.0%)
Return from Reduction of
Principle on Loan Balance: .... $ 9,000 (4.5%)
Annual Increase in Market
Value from 2% Appreciation: .... $ 20,000 (10.0%)
Total Return on Initial Equity
Down Payment of $200,000: .... $ 49,000 (24.5%)

I once sold several apartments to a married couple who purchased the property under terms like those illustrated above, except that they amortized the loan over 15 years, instead of 25. The increased loan payments left them with almost no cash flow, but in 15 short years the entire property would be free and clear of debt!

Two years later they walked past my door after a meeting with the property manager. I asked how their apartments were doing. They said, "Not very well. But that's O.K., how are you doing?" You couldn't meet two nicer people.

I reviewed their income and expenses, and they were consistent with our projections. Yet they were not pleased with their cash flow. Then it dawned on me! "Oh, I forgot," I said, "You have a 15-year loan." The wife looked at me and said, "No. No. We are paying this loan off in 7 years! We make extra payments on the loan each month."

Walking and Talking

I explained that the resulting negative cash flow, from making the extra payments, did not mean that the investment was a bad one. It was actually performing great! They burst out laughing that I would say something they considered to be so ridiculous. This caused me to start laughing, which of course, they found absolutely hysterical. There we all sat, laughing uncontrollably at each other. It was as if we were in the middle of a *Seinfeld* episode!

When I think back to that conversation it reminds me how differently people can view and interpret the same investment. This is because the motivations behind the ownership vary so widely from one investor to another. What might be a cash generator for one investor, is a retirement plan for another, and a college fund for yet another.

Conversations

KNOW YOUR LIMITS BUT DON'T LIMIT YOUR KNOWLEDGE

I once attended a real estate seminar regarding 1031 Like Kind Exchanges that lasted two full days. That is a lot of time to take away from a work week, but I wanted to be able to advise my clients on how to effectively utilize the exchange of real estate to defer the recapture of depreciation and the payment of capital gains tax. By the end of the class, I considered myself qualified to give advice on exchanges. The advice? Consult with your attorney and accountant.

Sometimes it is important to know what you don't know. On the flip side, if you learn everything you can about your product, you can often identify opportunities that you would otherwise not recognize. An example of this involved an investor I was working with who was exchanging an investment property he had owned for a long time, for a new $800,000 apartment building. He was going to use the $810,000 of proceeds from the first closing, being held in an escrow account, to pay "all-cash" for the apartment building. Having no loan on the property, his estimated cash flow was projected to be $70,000 per year.

Walking and Talking

Because this was an exchange of real estate, I knew from the seminar I had attended, that much of the $70,000 cash flow would be taxable, because his current depreciation schedule would only allow for a small portion of that cash flow to be tax-deferred.

I asked him, "Have you ever considered buying a second building? If you leveraged that building 100%, you would not generate any additional cash flow, but maybe you could use the depreciation from the second building to offset the $70,000 cash flow you are making on the first building. Ask your accountant if that makes any sense." (I always, always, always tell buyers and sellers that they must rely on their accountants and attorneys. They are the experts, I'm not!)

The following morning, he called me to say that he had talked with his accountant who agreed that it would be beneficial to purchase a second building and had decided to purchase a second building. Always refer your clients to the experts, but keep learning, so you can better recognize opportunities and ask the right questions.

Conversations

FLORIDA SHADE

To give you an idea of how long Berne Bratys has been selling real estate, let me just say that house lots in Florida were selling for $5,000. And that number included a lifetime golf membership!

Berne recalls one story that involved a dentist from Columbus who was interested in purchasing 9 Florida condominiums for investment property. The dentist gave Berne a 2-page list of items of concern he wanted dealt with before he would commit to the purchase. Berne met with the sellers, and then again with the dentist, and addressed each item to everyone's satisfaction. Then the dentist handed Berne another list!

"I met with the sellers again," says Berne, "and then scheduled a meeting with the buyer. At the beginning of our meeting, I told him to get his checkbook. He asked why, and I told him this was a no-nonsense meeting and that I was going to leave with a $52,000 earnest money check and a contract, or we just wouldn't have a deal. We had addressed his second page of requests. He was getting a great price due to the quantity he was buying. He wrote me the check."

A month later, the dentist decided he only wanted to keep 4 of the condominiums. However, because he had negotiated a great price, he stated that he was going to resell the 5 remaining condominiums himself and make a profit. Two months later the dentist called Berne in Florida to complain that while he was getting a lot of calls at his Columbus office, he couldn't get anyone to actually buy any of his five condominiums. Berne replied, "Don't feel bad Doc. I'm not doing very well filling teeth down here either."

The dentist decided to give the 5 remaining condos back to Berne to sell. Berne says, "He was a smart guy. One of the five he decided to give back was next to the pool, completely covered in shade from trees and a next-door high rise. You know, Garry, people buying a condo in Florida are doing so because they want sun! I wouldn't even show that one to prospects. Which just goes to show, you never know."

That condo in the shade ended up being the first one Berne sold. As he was showing condos to a vacationing couple, he was walking them past the pool area when the wife asked, "What about that one?" Berne told her that it was certainly available. She then said to her husband, "Look honey, we can sit on this side of the pool and go back and forth from the condo and still avoid the sun!" Berne's buyer had a sun allergy and they were absolutely thrilled!

Berne says, "We sold those condominiums for $55,000 in 1973 when lending was very tight. We were afraid that we might be overselling the promise of great appreciation. But, the market turned for the better, and within 4 years the condominiums were selling for over $100,000. Today they sell for a quarter million dollars. It just goes to show you never know."

More From The "Never Know" Department:

Five years ago Berne listed a two-family apartment building, sometimes referred to as a twin single. He sent the residents on both sides a letter explaining what a great opportunity they had to purchase the double, rent out one side, and live in the other. By leasing and managing the building themselves, they could limit expenses, build up equity from appreciation and principal reduction on the loan, and lower their monthly payment at the same time. What a deal! A week passed and Berne got no response.

So he drove out to the property to introduce himself and to explain that he would have to occasionally show the property to prospective buyers, making sure to post 24-hour notices on their doors before ever entering their apartment.

Berne recalls, "I knocked on the first door and when I explained this to the resident, he about threw me off his property. He screamed and yelled at me and told me to never come back. I actually thought he was about to take a swing at me."

A couple of days later, Berne got a call from a man who was responding to the letter Berne had sent about buying the double. It was the same guy!

After talking to him for several minutes Berne said, "Hey, by the way...remember that guy you screamed and yelled at the other day? That was me." The guy apologized up, down and sideways. Berne had probably just caught him on a bad day, because he ended up being a very likeable client. It just goes to show...

Walking and Talking

THE THREE-TWO PITCH

If you have ever been to the family-owned Plank's Cafe on Parson's Avenue in Columbus, you probably know the greatest bartender of all time, Jack Kelley. Jack doesn't really tend bar as much as he holds court. Whether the discussion turns to politics, current events or sports, Jack has an opinion, and that opinion is served up with a double order of flair, hold the onions. Plank's Cafe is the Cheers of Columbus, where everybody knows your name. Every time I seat myself at the lunch counter, Jack always looks at the person seated next to me (it never matters who that is), and says, "Do you know Scanny here? Great athlete, shortstop, weren't you Scanny? You know there were only two pitchers in the entire city who he couldn't hit.... a left handed pitcher and a right handed pitcher." He will then go on to explain that I couldn't hit the water if I fell out of the boat. So you can imagine my concern when I was thrown the following curve ball at a real estate closing early in my career.

It was a Friday afternoon on the last day of the month, and all of the loan documents and closing statements had been signed. As a formality, the title agent looked at the seller and asked, "And you, of course, are unmarried?"

The seller answered, "No, I'm married."

Everyone froze. Eyes began darting back and forth as everyone tried to find someone at the table who might not have an expression of shock, someone who could explain that the seller was only joking, or that we had known this all along and had already solved the obvious problem of dower rights. That someone was not in the room.

Not exactly sure why his last statement had caused such a sudden change of mood in the room, the seller tried to help the situation by adding, "But I haven't seen her for ten years, since she took off for Florida." Not quite the help we were looking for.

It was the first time I ever saw attorneys actually go through all of those books they keep on their shelves on the wall. I guess I always thought they were put there for decoration. As the three attorneys scoured through the books, and compared notes in hushed tones with each other, I was resigned to the fact that the deal would never close. Dower rights of the spouse are very strong and I couldn't imagine the title company insuring the ownership of the property without the wife's signature.

Sometimes I hear people say that closings are faster and simpler without an attorney present, but I have always found the opposite to be true. I have been at closings with dozens of different attorneys representing buyers and sellers. Some of the attorneys I already know, outstanding attorneys with great professional reputations like Ron Davis, Bill Diehl, Lewis DiRosario and Jeffrey Patter. There are other attorneys that I end up meeting for the first time at the closing table. In every case they bring with them an expertise that greatly facilitates the closing, and I am always glad they are there.

That Friday afternoon, I was especially glad they were there, because they arrived at a solution that satisfied all parties

Walking and Talking

and the transaction closed successfully. So, outside curve ball, hit to the opposite field for a triple. What do you think about that Jack!?

Author's Note:

Jack Kelley passed away in January of 2002, at the age of 69, after a brave and dignified battle with cancer.

A couple of weeks earlier, his nephew Tim Kelley and I visited with Jack and reminisced for a while. As often would happen, the conversation turned to sports. We talked about the time Jack scored 52 points in a basketball game and how sorry he felt for his teammates.

"Why did you feel sorry for your teammates?" Tim asked, knowing full-well the answer.

"Because I never passed them the ball!" Jack answered. "Poor guys."

"What happened when it was your turn to throw the inbounds pass?" I asked.

"I called time out!" Jack said.

Sometimes a friend's passing can cause you to consider the single quality you most admired about that person. Jack was truly blessed with the ability to make people laugh and to make them feel better about themselves. Anyone who spent time with Jack left with a smile. This was true to the end, when at the gravesite, his friends and family said a prayer and then sang a rendition of Jack's favorite song, "Take Me Out To The Ballgame!" One more smile on everyone's face as Jack rounded third and headed for home. He will be missed.

Conversations

ALL IN THE FAMILY

Until I wrote this collection of stories, I never stopped to consider how many of my friends and family are in the business of real estate. My father Jim Scanlon sells investment real estate, my brother Dan and his wife Kathy sell residential homes, and my wife Sherri is an expert in the marketing of new construction condominiums. Sherri's side of the family is chock-full of uncles, brothers, and cousins who sell, lease and construct real estate, as does her father Jim Thomas, of J.E. Thomas Development Company.

Jim Thomas has built just about every type of real estate. He is considered one of Central Ohio's premier builders of midsize medical office buildings. Jim and his wife Doris are very athletic. One evening, after playing three sets of tennis with Jim and Doris (I later discovered they had ridden twenty miles on their bicycles before our tennis match), Jim told me a funny story over dinner.

Jim had just completed the construction of a large apartment community. This was during the gas shortage of the late 70's when the expert advice out of the White House was predicting the virtual depletion of all gas by the year 2000. There was a moratorium placed on supplying any new apartments with gas heat, requiring the alternative use of propane gas. A huge, thirty foot tank of propane gas was delivered and installed next to the apartments. Jim said, "It looked like a giant submarine coming down the street when they trucked it to the site."

"The same day the tank was installed, I was meeting with another client about a mile away," Jim recalls, "when all of a sudden we heard this gigantic BOOM!"

"We were both startled. Since the sound had come from the direction of the huge tank that had just been installed, I thought the worst," Jim said.

Jim never did find out the source of that "BOOM"; fortunately, it was not the propane tank. Within a year or so, the ban on gas heat was lifted and the buyers had the property retrofitted with gas heat. Jim laughs, "But I will never forget the feeling I had that day."

Conversations

WALKING THE HALL WAY

In his 1st twenty years as an office specialist, John Hall has leased or sold over 10 million square feet of downtown and suburban office space, representing over $800 million dollars of transaction volume. This has earned John "Midwest Commercial Broker All Star" status from Mid-America Real Estate Magazine.

After graduating from The Ohio State University with a marketing degree, John first worked as a data base coordinator before beginning his sales and leasing career with Planned Communities.

John recalls, "Jay and Tod Ortlip (the owners of Planned Communities) said they would not offer me any formal training, but they promised to answer any questions I had along the way. So every week I would go through my list of questions."

One of the questions was, "Can they really do that?"

"It was one of the first large transactions I ever worked on. I had worked on the deal for several months and the commission was going to be almost $60,000. Three days before the closing, the buyer's wife filed for divorce and froze all of their assets.

'Can you really do that?' I asked. Obviously, it wasn't the answer I wanted to hear. I spent 2 years with Tom and Jay, who taught me a lot, and were always friendly and helpful."

In 1988 John joined CB Commercial Real Estate Group. It was during his first year with CB that John experienced one of his most memorable deals. A deal that fell apart.

"I was searching for 2,500 square feet of space for Sterling Software. I put in a lot of time working to find them the best spot. In the end, however, they decided on another location that I hadn't shown them, which was a disappointment. But soon after that, Sterling Software called to say they were looking for another site, and since I had worked so hard for them before, they thought I deserved another shot. That other shot ended up being an assignment to locate a 60,000 square foot space. Ultimately, they decided on 100,000 square feet. That was my first large transaction," John says.

This is just one more example of building a relationship by earning the respect of clients that result in solid business, and John has been doing that for two decades. And relationships are always changing. John changed companies from CB to Columbus Commercial Realty (CCR) in 1994. In 2005, however, CB, now named CB Richard Ellis Inc. acquired CCR. So John is now back with CB, proving that the more things change, the more things stay the same.

Conversations

YOU OUGHT TO BE AN ARCHITECT!

As he rode his bicycle to his job at the grocery store, on a warm day in July of 1965, Bill Riat, like a lot of high school kids his age, was largely unaware to what extent he would be impacted by the influences of his childhood, beginning with those of his parents.

Bill's father John, a Bronze Star recipient of World War II, had fought in the infamous Battle of the Bulge in December of 1944. During that battle the German Army advanced on the American troops forming a bulge in the line. It was soon discovered that vital maps showing terrains and locations had been left behind in a farmhouse previously used by the Americans. John Riat and 3 other volunteers from his unit raced back in a jeep, behind German lines, to retrieve the maps. He was the only soldier to survive the return trip through enemy territory.

After the war, John married Ursula Clarke (affectionately nicknamed Dodo), and together they set up their household on the South side of Columbus. John worked as a welder and Dodo was the secretary to Monsignor Schwendeman who was in charge of overseeing the building of a new church for Christ the

King Parish. Bill's mother was responsible for keeping track of incoming bills and preparing the checks for the monsignor to sign.

Bill recalls, "Throughout construction of the church, Mom kept writing these big checks to an architect in New York. And she knew that I enjoyed the mechanical drawing classes I was taking at Hartley High School. So, while I thought I could be a draftsman, she would always tell me that I ought to become an architect. All through my high school years she would say, 'You can be an architect', or 'You'll make a great architect.' I thought it was funny."

During those years, Bill worked for Leo Deitline, the store manager of the busiest Kroger Grocery store in Columbus.

Bill says, "Everything was done for 'Mrs. Smith'. We always referred to our average customer as 'Mrs. Smith'. We would bag the groceries, wheel them outside, and load up the car for her. If someone asked for a particular item that we didn't have in stock, instead of simply telling the customer we were out of that product, Mr. Deitline would say that he would check the inventory in back. Then, he would give me a few bucks and send me to the Super Duper two blocks down the street. When I returned he would scrape off their sticker and replace it with one of ours. He never wanted to disappoint a customer. When you see the customer loyalty that results from that high standard of customer service, it stays with you your entire life."

Bill continued to work 30 hours per week while attending The Ohio State University.

By their sophomore year, OSU students were required to declare a major.

"When they asked me," Bill says, "I really didn't know what to say, but I had remembered what my mom had always said , so I answered that I wanted to be an architect. After listening to her all of those years, it just seemed natural."

Conversations

Initially, Bill's announcement was met with some discouragement. "Since I was one of the few students who actually had to work during school to even afford the architectural fraternity, some teachers suggested that I should select another major. The dean at that time actually said, 'You probably will not make it here.' It gave me serious pause and almost caused me to second-guess whether or not I could make the grade. But I was determined to try."

During Bill's senior year, Bill gave new meaning to the term 'getting by on a dime'. Bill married his wife, Sheila, and together they lived for 3 months in Switzerland, on a student exchange program.

Bill recalls, "Thirty students went to Switzerland that year, and to a person, each one would tell you that it absolutely changed their lives. We became lifelong friends with Pierre Zolly and his wife, the couple who founded the program, and we returned every couple of years to visit them. It was on that first trip, however, that our perspective on the world really blossomed. Before that, neither of us had ever even been on an airplane. It allowed us to see other parts of the world on a very thin budget. We literally had things planned down to a dime. At the end of our trip we had enough money for 2 Cokes, 2 hot dogs, and a dime to make a phone call from the airport for someone to pick us up. We arrived home with 9 cents in our pocket!"

And Bill developed a love for architecture. "I really enjoy the creative energy that goes into building something entirely new; something that is not already there yet. There is always some risk involved when you build something from nothing, so you will always encounter the naysayers. But, one of my favorite quotes is by Albert Einstein who said, 'Great spirits have always encountered violent opposition from mediocre minds.' That is why it is so important to surround yourself with positive people who share the same goals and dream the same

Walking and Talking

dreams as you."

One of Bill's first projects after graduation, while working for architect Jim Monsul, was to help design Pickerington Square Shopping Center for developer Dick Solove.

"That is where I met Dick Solove, Don Kelley, Bob Weiler, and Don Casto. I learned so much from them. Obviously, they had extraordinary business prowess, but what made them unique was the way they conducted business. Every meeting we had, they would first spend time talking about personal matters. Most people go straight to business. But with them, you always looked forward to the meetings, because it was so much fun. One of the reasons they continue to accomplish so much is because they receive so much cooperation from everyone they work with. They let you have fun while working on their projects. Even their expertise is secondary to their passion, their friendliness, and their enthusiasm."

A few years after college, Bill helped found Newtowne Homes, specializing in the design and construction of single family homes. Soon thereafter, interest rates rose to 22% for construction loans and a 30-year fixed rate loan for homebuyers reached 17%. That is when another influence from Bill's childhood re-emerged; his bicycle.

"The market was difficult for everyone during those years of high interest rates in the late 70's and early 80's. I would ride my bike 15 to 20 miles, out in the country. It was a great stress reliever. It provided some quiet time and a great workout. It was a good way to blow off some steam and deal with the frustrations of a stalled marketplace. It really helped me keep things in their proper perspective."

The slow times taught Bill some important lessons, including the importance of solving problems quickly, as soon as things appear to be going in the wrong direction. "Confront each problem immediately; try to nip it in the bud," Bill says. "Oftentimes the tendency is to procrastinate and wait too long to take necessary action."

But Bill believes that the best lessons come from experiencing things that go well.

"After Newtowne dissolved, I began working for myself, but soon realized that I did not want to be a lone wolf. Remembering the experience I had with Dick, Don, Bob and Don, taught me that if you surround yourself with people you enjoy and trust you will be happy. And the by-product of being happy at your work is that you also become successful. By partnering with the people at CASTO, I am able to work across the entire spectrum of planning, financing, construction, property management, and sales. I work with land owners, city officials, partners, lenders, architects, engineers, and appraisers. It's wonderful working with an entire team of people," Bill says.

In this business what goes around, comes around. Today, one of the many projects Bill is working on, in partnership with CASTO, is the re-development of the very shopping center, Pickerington Square, he first worked on as an architect straight out of school. The initial buildings he designed are being demolished and replaced with a new Giant Eagle grocery store that will, no doubt, implement the same strategies of customer service that Leo Deitline taught Bill years ago.

And the bicycle is still in service. Now riding regularly with his son John, the two of them biked The Tour of the Scioto River Valley, a 2-day, 200 mile bicycle tour between Columbus and Portsmouth on this year's Mother's Day. It was an appropriate day to remember the influence a mother had on a son when she suggested, "You ought to be an architect." The Ohio State University's College of Engineering and School of Architecture concurred by presenting Bill with a 2005 Distinguished Alumnus Award.

Walking and Talking

6

Stories of Risk and Reward

Walking and Talking

Stories of Risk and Reward

"If you can make one heap of all your winnings,
And risk it on one turn of pitch-and-toss,
And lose, and start again at your beginnings,
And never breathe a word about your loss."
                                    Rudyard Kipling

"The people I want to hear about are the people who take risks."
                                    Robert Frost

Stories of Risk and Reward is a collection of stories that show how the real estate world of business is so entwined with high risk and high reward. Real estate is an entrepreneurial field where time, money and energy are always put at risk in hopes of achieving long-term success.

Following are stories of risk and reward…

Walking and Talking

7 11 12 14 28 32

For Kevin Clay the worst day of his professional life also happens to be the best day of his professional life. On February 23, 1989, Kevin was informed that the huge, national health care corporation he worked for was making cutbacks. His services were no longer necessary. Kevin was laid off...let go...fired!

It was not as if Kevin really enjoyed his job as a computer programmer. The pay was very low, and the hours of inputting line after line of computer commands were long and boring. However, the thought of being out of work for the first time in his life was a traumatic one. And since he had also parted ways with his longtime girlfriend earlier that week Kevin was not in the greatest of moods. It was on impulse that Kevin decided to play the lottery at a convenience store that day.

It was only a small risk to take. Kevin called out six numbers, none with any special meaning, just those that came to mind. To this day he cannot even remember which six numbers he picked, but he insists that he was not surprised when the winning numbers were announced... and they did not match a single number on his ticket. He had lost his girlfriend, then his

Stories of Risk and Reward

job, and finally, the lottery! Not a good day, he thought.

But it actually turned out to be a very fortunate day for Kevin. Being laid off from a boring job that he considered "safe and secure" forced him to consider other career paths that he otherwise would have considered too risky. With his newfound knowledge that any job could be lost in an instant, the 100% straight commission aspect of commercial real estate sales was no longer as scary to him as it had once been. So he decided to take the risk of pursuing a career in real estate, where the rewards would be higher if he worked hard and succeeded.

Fast-forward two years. Kevin and I were going over the final details of his first large-volume real estate sale - a 32,000 square-foot retail shopping center. He had worked on the retail center for over a year, and stood to earn a commission equal to a year's pay at his old job. He had a lot of time, effort and income at stake.

In real estate sales, good fortune can play a major role. There are many things beyond the control of the sales agent: interest rates can go up, zonings can be denied and so on. Often we have to hope for good fortune. We hope the timing is right and the outside conditions work to our advantage. The old adage "it is better to be lucky than good" can often seem true in this business.

The following day Kevin was both fortunate and successful. The property sold, Kevin earned a well-deserved commission and was on his way to a very successful career.

Four years after his first sale, Kevin decided to specialize to a large degree, in locating land sites for development. This actually involved quite a lot of risk, because he needed to commit all of his time to learning about land development, locating particular sites and overseeing the steps necessary to get the transaction closed. Since it can often take as long as one to two years to go from making a purchase offer on land to sitting down

Walking and Talking

at a closing table, you can commit a lot of time and energy without knowing if things will work out in your favor. Your success depends on lenders, appraisers, wetland studies, soil studies, survey reports, zoning regulations, utility easements, title issues and a myriad of other factors over which you have little control. Which brings us to Lucy's farm.

Lucy's farm consisted of 34 acres that required all of the usual studies necessary for the buyer to proceed to closing. After being in contract for six months, Kevin's buyers needed the seller to grant them eight additional months to close the transaction. Otherwise, the contract would expire before the buyers could obtain the changes in zoning that were necessary to justify the negotiated sale price. Lucy, the seller, agreed to grant the extension of time on one condition: she must be paid $1,000 per month for the extension of time. After eight months, if the zoning was turned down, the contract would be terminated and Lucy would keep the $8,000.

"The buyer flatly refused and we were at a standstill," Kevin remembers. "I considered paying the $1,000 per month myself! If the deal closed successfully, I would receive a sizeable commission. However, if one of a dozen possible problems occurred, problems that were outside of my control, then the deal would be canceled and I would have to pay the $8,000 price of the extension. It was a particularly difficult decision to make because I didn't have a lot of savings built up in my bank account! I decided to take the risk. I believed in the deal and that the odds were in my favor."

This particular risk resulted in one of the largest earned commissions in Kevin's career. It provided Kevin the means to continue his goal of specializing in land acquisition. Today, Kevin is one of the premier land acquisition specialists in Central Ohio. While he continues to advise his clients on investment real estate, his specialty involves locating available land for office, retail, residential and multifamily development. He walks and talks with developers, sellers, zoning officials, attorneys, architects and neighborhood representatives to plan and zone land for its highest value and best use.

Kevin's decision to enter 100% commission sales and to pay $8,000 for Lucy's farm deal demonstrates that risk and good fortune do not always come in the form of a lottery ticket.

Walking and Talking

5 14 17 35 36 41

Wednesday, February 22nd, Pete Coratola did what he had done every Wednesday for the previous 2 years. He played the lottery.

Pete, a police officer, was working special duty at a bank to earn additional income. Every Wednesday, during his lunch break, Pete would spend ten dollars on the lottery. He would pay nine dollars for a ticket with 9 numbers. He would then take his last dollar and "pool" it with 8 other employees at the bank who would each give Pete one dollar.

So Pete purchased 2 tickets, each with nine numbers. Nine chances to win on each ticket.

Pete returned to the bank, reached into his pocket and pulled out the 2 tickets. Haphazardly, he put one ticket into the vault at the bank (this would be the "pool" ticket), and put the other ticket into his wallet (this would be Pete's ticket).

At nine o'clock the following morning, Pete woke up and answered the ringing telephone. The five bank tellers, the two managers and the other special duty police officer that worked at the bank were laughing and screaming at Pete, telling him that he had won the lottery. Pete hung up on them.

Pete recalls that morning. "The second time they called I hung up again. When they called back the third time, I really thought they had taken the joke a little too far, so I hung up the phone and then took it off the hook! I figured they had all had their laughs, and I went back to sleep."

An hour later Pete's doorbell rang, and the fellow police officer at the door told Pete that he had really won the lottery. Pete called the lottery commission, confirmed the winning number, rented a limousine, picked up everyone from the bank and drove to the lottery commission.

"It really was cool the way it all happened," Pete says. "They had me place the ticket into this machine and when I did, lights went on and the number '$9,000,000' lit up."

What are the odds that he would buy the winning ticket? Or that the winnings would be exactly $9 million dollars to be divided by a group of nine? Or that he would have two tickets, each with 9 numbers? Or that he would put one ticket in his wallet, and the other ticket (that ended up having the winning number) in the bank vault for the group?

I asked Pete if he ever thought about the fact that if he had put the winning ticket into his wallet he would have been the sole winner of all $9 million dollars.

"Oh sure," Pete answered. "But it's hard to feel unlucky when you have just won a million dollars. It all worked out for the best." What Pete did next is another story...

EASY STREET?

My guess is that most people who win the lottery look upon their good fortune as an avenue for an easier life. Many end up quitting their jobs. Pete Coratola decided to add another job to the one he already had!

Pete, a ten year veteran police officer, looked upon his windfall as an opportunity to get involved in something that had always interested him: real estate.

Some people might be inclined to think, "Oh sure...now that he is a millionaire he can buy all the real estate he wants." But in reality, his winnings did not make him rich. The million-dollar payout was scheduled to be paid to Pete in increments of $50,000 per year for 20 years. After tax, Pete would be paid $35,000 per year. With this amount added to his income as a police officer, Pete was comfortable, but certainly not in as high of an income bracket as are thousands of doctors, dentists, attorneys, business owners, etc. So Pete feels fortunate that John Dragoo took a chance on him.

"It was my first real estate investment," Pete recalls. "I wanted to purchase 33 apartments for $620,000, but I didn't have

Stories of Risk and Reward

the 20% downpayment, so I asked John to take back a note from me for $125,000 that he could secure with a second mortgage on the property. John asked me why in the world he should take a chance on loaning me that much money. I said, 'John, I'm a police officer, I drive a Chevy truck, and I eat apple pie. What's more American than that?!' " Pete continued, "John Dragoo lent me the money, and from there I continued to invest in apartments. If John had turned me down, who knows what would have happened? I am not even sure I would have continued to pursue real estate. Since that time, I have purchased over $100 million of real estate and have never had to come out of pocket for the downpayment."

Pete uses "intense, hands-on property management" to enhance the value of the real estate he buys; to build equity. Then he uses that equity to finance additional apartments. He explained to me over lunch how he and John Beggs (you will learn more about John Beggs later in the book) were able to apply their management style to the four different apartment communities I sold them, to generate strong cash flow, build equity and leverage into other profitable properties. It was then that I suggested he pick up the lunch check. (It's all about timing.)

Today, Pete owns Platinum Management. He owns and develops hotels, water parks, car washes, and office buildings.

"Luck" can come in many forms, from taking a chance on a lottery ticket, to having someone take a chance on you. From buying a lottery ticket while working his second job at the bank, to adding a second career after he won the lottery, Pete demonstrates that the harder you work, the "luckier" you get.

Walking and Talking

PULL!

In the business world, most of us base our relationships with clients and associates on observations we make of each other during the work week. However, you can often learn as much, or more, about a person by the way he or she plays. This is certainly true in the case of John Beggs.

John invited me, along with a couple of his friends, to shoot skeet at a club he had recently joined. I looked forward to trying something I had never done before.

John opened up the back hatch of his sports utility vehicle and handed each of us a shotgun, earplugs, ammo and a vest - all top-line equipment. John explained the basics of the sport with us and patiently answered all of our questions as we walked to the range to shoot at the projected clay targets. We were also able to learn by listening to his conversations with the other members who were also out that particular afternoon enjoying their favorite sport. We soon learned that, despite being relatively new to the sport, John could flat-out shoot!

As to my performance, let me just say that nobody was hurt and they assured me that with a little bit of spackle and

Stories of Risk and Reward

paint the corner of the barn would soon be as good as new.

It was classic John Beggs: gracious, prepared, intense and focused. He had discovered a new interest he was passionate about and wanted to introduce the activity to his friends. That day I discovered that John played as hard as he worked.

John is both a lawyer and an accountant. He was an owner of a large diamond and gold retail chain when he decided to expand into the purchase of investment real estate. Pete Coratola, the police officer who hit the lottery while working special duty at one of his locations, expressed the same interest to John. After they formed a partnership to buy apartments, I sold them their first joint venture, a 52-unit apartment community, and have since sold them several other investment properties.

John's legal and accounting skills were put to use towards the financing, tax work, and contract issues involved in real estate. Pete focused on organizing the property management staff, handling the leasing, etc. In less than seven years they accumulated over 1,500 apartments in Ohio.

One time, Pete and John signed a contract to purchase 110 townhome apartments. Because the apartments were not producing the amount of income typically expected from such a property, they negotiated a contract for a lower-than-normal purchase price, with the added contingency that they be able to inspect the inside of each apartment.

The day of the property inspection, they were careful to give the apartments a thorough review. After they had been shown 80% of the apartments, the leasing agent began walking back to the rental office.

"We are not through," Pete said. "We have not inspected all of the apartments."

"Oh, yes, I'm sorry," she said as she changed directions and began fumbling at her ring of keys. "I forgot about the others. Probably because I have been told not to lease them."

The remaining 20% of the apartments were in excellent condition, rent-ready for new residents. John and Pete never found out why the apartments had been left unavailable for rent. A cynical person might come to the conclusion that the property management company intentionally left them vacant so the property, which had been listed for sale for over two years, would never reach high enough income numbers to attract a buyer. And they in turn would not lose the management income. Whatever the reason, John and Pete closed on the property, leased all 20 of the vacant apartments within two months and ended up with extraordinary cash flow from the property.

John Beggs' success in real estate came as no suprise to me. Nor was I surprised when, after only 2 years of involving himself in the sport of skeet shooting, he won the 1997 World Skeet Shooting Double Championship. John works and plays to win.

Stories of Risk and Reward

MEETING MRS. CLAUS

I asked John Beggs what initially got him interested in real estate.

"While going to school at Penn State I visited some friends at a home that had been converted into a boarding house for students. The landlord was a friendly lady by the name of Mrs. Claus who spoke with a thick German accent. My friend was paying $80 per month for a bedroom and the right to share a bath down the hall with 7 other students who had the same arrangement," John said.

It didn't take John long to multiply 8 students x $80 x 12 months.

John remembers, "Total rent was $7,680 per year, and at the time, the house itself was only worth $20,000! I didn't know anything about depreciation or capital gains or leverage, but it was very apparent that something exciting was happening."

John purchased his first double in 1981 in Fairborn, and still owns it to this day.

"I borrowed money to buy the property, and since then I have paid it off twice and refinanced twice. The last refinance paid the college tuition for my oldest son and the high school tuition for my middle son," says John.

Today John owns and manages 1,160 apartments. While many investors are hesitant to enter into partnerships, John has always enjoyed purchasing real estate with other investors. John says, "Partners keep me from getting too wound up in a deal. Bouncing ideas off of other investors, who have a stake in the transaction, forces me to look at things from a variety of perspectives."

Risky Business:

I asked John what his riskiest venture was. After remembering that John served as an infantryman during the Vietnam War, I specified "investment" venture. "That's easy... sixty-eight apartments on Cleveland Avenue. Two of the buildings were completely vacant and two were half empty. In one apartment, the resident left without bothering to take their pet dog with them. Everything was a complete mess and it was going to require very intense management. However, at a price of $7,000 per apartment in the mid-1990's, we wondered how we could go wrong. But we were less experienced at the time and considered it to be a big risk. We paid $480,000, put $50,000 of improvements into the property and sold it 2 years later for $980,000."

Mrs. Claus would be proud.

DEALING WITH UNCERTAINTY

A friend of mine, who is a government employee, knows with virtual certainty that if he goes to work every day for the next week he will be paid for his effort. In fact, he is able to calculate exactly what percentage of his income he will receive in the form of a pension if he works until age 58, age 60, or age 65. If he works overtime he can tell you to the penny how he will be compensated on an hourly basis. Even if he is sick for 3 or 4 days and can't go to work, he knows exactly how much he will earn for sick time. He also knows exactly how much pay he gets for vacation time.

One of the most difficult aspects of 100% commission sales is dealing with the uncertainty that your efforts will result in compensation. Every time I see a sales agent spending hundreds of hours on a single transaction over the course of several months, I know that he or she is keenly aware that they might not be paid a dime for their time, effort and expertise. Some agents spread out this risk by spending their time on a larger number of smaller transactions in hopes that at least some of them will close and they will receive some compensation.

It takes a very positive attitude to remain self-motivated for days or weeks on end, working on something that you know has a high probability of "becoming null and void and of no effect in contract or equity." When a deal falls apart, you consider all of the time you spent on the deal. You think about the weekends of wonderful weather you spent at the office, the outlay of money spent on overnight mailings, long distance phone calls, gasoline, etc. It is hard to gear up for the next "possible" deal.

However, sometimes ignorance is bliss. For instance, in retrospect it was probably a good thing that our group of commercial Realtors did not know in 1986 that the tax benefits of owning investment real estate were going to be eliminated by a drastic change in the tax code. Or that this would result in a 20% decrease in property values, and that lenders would stop lending, sellers would stop selling, lessees would stop leasing, and the savings and loan industry would experience a crisis. Despite all of this, an extraordinary number of these agents went on to become outstanding leaders in their field.

The nature of real estate is that there is a lot of uncertainty. Uncertainty creates both fear and hope. Fear that all might be for naught. Hope that every effort and every risk will be rewarded. Reality lies somewhere in between. So does good fortune, opportunity and perseverance. What a great business!

7

Stories of Technology

Walking and Talking

Stories of Technology

"I never did anything worth doing by accident, nor did any of my inventions come by accident, they came by work."

Thomas Edison

Some people use technology in the wrong way. For instance, they often "hide" behind e-mail to keep from interacting face-to-face with professionals in their field. Other people ignore new technology out of a fear of change. Likewise, they do not always make the best use of the technology that is available to them.

The following **Stories of Technology** point out how technology can be an outstanding tool to leverage our efforts…

I HAVE CARRIED A COMPUTER IN MY POCKET FOR 20 YEARS!

If I had to single out the most important tool available to me when I entered the world of investment real estate, without a doubt it would be the Hewlett Packard 38 C financial calculator (now replaced with the slimmer version called the *hp* 12C). I believe it is the single most empowering tool available to a commercial real estate agent. I will never forget the day in 1982 when I noticed Bill Daniel, a co-worker and mentor of mine, making calculations on this hand-held calculator that was so far ahead of its time.

Soon, Bill was teaching me how to use it to calculate monthly payments, amortization schedules, internal rates of return, future values of cash flows, balloon payments and blend-rate financing. I couldn't believe it! And to top it off, it fit in my coat pocket. I was immediately excited to test its practical use on applications of all kinds. As I learned how to work the calculator, I also achieved a greater appreciation and understanding of the time-value of money. It was self-teaching!

You cannot have breakfast with a group of commercial brokers without someone pulling out their *hp* 12C to analyze a deal they're discussing. I don't know how many times I've heard the phrase, "Hey, do you have an *hp* on you I can borrow?" If they are offered anything else but an *hp*, they will just say "Never mind."

Today, I actually own three *hp* 12C calculators. They weigh less than seven ounces. Usually, I keep one at the office, one at home, and one in my briefcase or coat pocket. My wife, Sherri, also has one, and I have given them to nephews, nieces and friends, and as prizes to students in the Junior Achievement class. I recommend to everyone interested in learning more about investments that they learn to use the *hp* 12C. The best words to describe the benefit of using the *hp* 12C are personal empowerment.

I received a phone call a few months ago from a friend of mine to whom I had sold four apartments two years earlier. He and his wife were considering refinancing the loan on their apartments.

As John described his recent phone conversation with a lender who had quoted him a 7.25% interest rate with no points, I reached into the desk drawer where I keep a copy of all my closing folders. I retrieved his closing statement where I had written the interest rate and amortization term of the buyer's loan.

I punched the original loan amount of $175,000 into the present value key (PV), the monthly interest rate (9.0%/12 months) into the interest rate key (i), 360 months into the number of months key (n), and then hit the payment key (PMT). Instantly, the *hp* 12C calculated the monthly payment at $1,408. I stored this result on key 1 of the calculator. As I asked John what amount the lender had quoted him for appraisal fees and closing fees, I punched in 24 months (for the length of time he had owned the property) and punched the future value key (FV).

135

Walking and Talking

Before John was able to answer that they had quoted him approximately $900 for those items, the *hp* 12C had calculated his current loan balance to be $172,497.

"Well, John, your current loan balance is $172,497," I said.

"How do you know that?" he replied.

"I have an *hp* calculator," I said. "Now if you add the $900 closing fees to your current loan balance, your new loan amount will be $173,397. Your new payment at 7.25% will be about $1,183, saving you $225 per month. So, your payback period on your $900 closing fees is 4 months. You might want to consider converting over to a new 15-year loan. Your payments will increase to $1583 per month, which will increase your current monthly payment by $175, but you will have the entire loan paid off in 15 years instead of 30!"

"What if I want to keep the payments the same? How long at today's rate would it take to pay off the loan?" He said.

I punched $1,408 into the PMT button, and pushed the N button.

"227 months; or just under 19 years. Maybe you should consider a 20-year loan," I said. Being able to take advantage of the *hp* 12C creates a lot of credibility with your clients. You are of more service to them. I use the *hp* 12C to review every investment I make, whether it is in real estate or another venture. It is truly invaluable.

This summer I plan on actually paying our kids, as an incentive, to read the instruction book and learn the *hp*. (Yes, there will be an exam!) It will be one of the least expensive, most valuable financial educations they will receive.

Thank you, Bill Daniel.

Stories of Technology

KNOWING TECHNOLOGY
(YOURS AND THEIRS)

     I once learned a very important lesson about supervising the remarkable technology that today's businesses use. My computer was open to the database program I use to access the names, addresses, and phone numbers of various clients, accountants, attorneys, appraisers, lenders, etc. With a dozen things to get done by the end of the day, I typed in the name of a seller's attorney. The computer then merged the attorney's name and number onto a fax cover letter. All I had to do was add to the letter the names and numbers of everyone involved with the sale, and attach a copy of the signed contract for one of my largest sales of the year. I hit the print key, signed the letter, added the contract, and fired it off! It seemed so efficient!

     Then I realized I had made a mistake and had sent the fax to another commercial real estate agent who had the same exact name as the seller's attorney. The computer had done its job. I just hadn't double-checked to make sure that only one contact in my database matched the criteria I had typed in. Fortunately, the other agent was very ethical and called me to say he had received the fax, understood the mistake and would keep everything confidential. The result could have been a lot worse. Now I try to better supervise the technology I use.

It is also important to understand how others are using technology. I was on the telephone one day with an investor from the state of Washington, explaining the apartment market in Columbus, Ohio. He seemed to be very familiar with every aspect of the local market that I was discussing. When I offhandedly mentioned the school district of one of the apartment communities we had for sale, he said, "I know." I replied, "How do you know that?"

He explained how he had, "spent a lot of time researching the apartments on the Internet."

While surfing the net, he had learned all about our company, had brought up comparable sales from the county courthouse records, navigated through all of the rent magazine websites to learn about rent rates, features and concessions being offered in Columbus. He had done a virtual walkthrough of the interiors of our apartments and had scoured through local neighborhood and business magazines to read about current events regarding the economic and business growth of the city. In some ways, he was more current on local activity than I was.

From clear across the country, he and his wife decided to purchase several apartments. Only for the closing itself, did they consider it necessary to actually visit Columbus and physically see the apartments. Any guesses on how they ordered their tickets?

Not only did this experience remind me to always consider, how I can make better use of available technology, but also how others are making use of it, too.

Stories of Technology

IT WAS 4%...DO YOU COPY?

Recently, at a closing of a six-family apartment building, the closing agent asked everyone at the table if they would be so kind as to use a pen with blue ink.

He said, "The photocopiers they have today are too good! When we take the documents to the courthouse to have them recorded, it is almost impossible to determine the signed originals from the copies. Therefore, if you use blue ink, we can easily identify the originals."

This reminded me of the $1,400 lesson I received during my first year in real estate. I was delivering a real estate purchase offer from a married couple wanting to buy a newly constructed home. When I presented the offer to the seller's agent, he said, "I see you have a real estate commission of 3% to be paid to your company. We are currently paying 4%." He immediately drew a line through the "3%", wrote in "4%" and initialed the change. It didn't take me long to calculate that an extra 1% of a $140,000 home was $1,400. Yeh boy!

At the closing four weeks later, I must admit, I was probably more concerned with shaking everyone's hand and making a good impression than with keeping a close eye on the closing documents, which of course is what I should have been doing. After the closing, I threw the commission check and all of the paperwork in my briefcase and returned to the office.

While making copies, I looked at the commission check. $4,200? 3%?! What?! I checked the contract. There it was, 4%, plain as day. I called the seller's agent immediately and explained the mistake.

"I'm sorry Garry, but the contract clearly says 3%," he said.

"Something is wrong," I said. "I'll be right over."

When I arrived, I took one look at the contract and realized what had happened. There was a faint line of whiteness that ran through the "3%" and that was all. Their copier did not pick up blue ink. So, when he drew the line and wrote his initials, in blue ink, on the original, their photocopy showed none of the changes.

Did I mention that the homebuilder was going through some thin economic times? In light of their cash troubles, the builder asked if they could pay the additional 1% at a later time, as a professional courtesy. Their plea was an honest one, so I agreed. Unfortunately, for them and for me, they liquidated their business and our brokerage was never paid the extra 1%. That lesson taught me to check both the copies and the originals of the agreements. Even if you have everything well documented and everyone agrees with you on a particular issue, it is always more difficult to get things straightened out after the fact.

Stories of Technology

WITH THE TOUCH OF A BUTTON

Jim Garrett is Senior VP of Client Services for NAI, one of the world's largest commercial brokerages. Jim is always on the cutting edge of the newest technology in the real estate market. He is a tremendous communicator who understands the practical ways in which technology can be applied to achieve tangible results for his sales agents. Jim was working with a very talented landlord broker in the San Francisco Bay area, who, at the time, was competing against the nation's largest commercial brokerages for a contract to market and sell a $49 million office park under construction. The broker was scheduled to be the last person, over a four-day period, to present his marketing proposal.

The broker discovered that several other brokers were using Microsoft PowerPoint as a presentation tool, which is exactly what he had planned to do. So, he contacted Jim Garrett for advice on how he could somehow differentiate himself from his competition.

Jim replied "Why don't you build a web site and use it as your presentation?" Today it is becoming commonplace to incorporate web sites in the marketing of a property, but in the

Walking and Talking

mid 90's it was still a relatively new concept. The broker seized the idea and, over the next few days, developed a 15-page web site at a cost of $2,500. The web site featured floor plans, artist renderings, lease terms, local amenities, etc.

The broker and his team walked into the meeting and addressed the decision makers around the table. "I know that you've interviewed the best office brokers in the city, and that each one gave great reasons why you should choose them to market your property. I bet they all estimated that it would take 14 to 16 weeks to get the product in front of all the potential buyers and tenants in San Francisco. Am I right?" He asked. They all agreed.

Then he looked around the room and in a quiet tone asked "What is the estimated carrying cost for 16 weeks on a $48 million dollar project?" One person at the table began working on his *hp* 12C, but everyone knew the number he would arrive at would be very high. One million dollars? Maybe more.

The broker gave a very impressive demonstration of his web site. Then, he paused. He punched in a telephone number on his cell phone, looked at the developers and said, "I can call my assistant and have her post this website on the Internet. She will then forward the Executive Summary via e-mail to over 5,000 commercial brokers worldwide. In minutes, we can save on your carrying cost and notify brokers from around the world, not just around the Bay Area, about your property, if you endorse this agreement and give me the exclusive right to market your property for 120 days."

He walked out of that meeting with an approved listing agreement, and a check for $120,000 to use towards marketing the property. Billboards that advertised the web site surrounded the property fronting on major highways. Within nine months of the office park's completion, they reached 93% occupancy. Jim Garrett is quick to point out that it required a lot of skill and hard work, but it all started with the knowledge of the very latest technology available and the simple touch of a button.

Walking and Talking

Developing Stories

"I just got fantastic news from my real estate agent in Florida. They found land on my property."
  Milton Berle

Developers bring unique skills to the real estate world. They are able to work with land planners, city administrators, zoning attorneys, accountants, lenders, surveyors, construction companies, investors, attorneys, accountants, and real estate agents to transform a raw piece of land into a shopping center, an apartment community, an office building, or an industrial park. They dream big and act on their dreams.

Here are their **Developing Stories...**

Walking and Talking
___

GET A HOBBY!

 John W. Messmore's education in the world of high finance began at the young age of 14, when he asked his father if he could borrow $250 to buy a motor scooter. His father's response was, "If you want it bad enough, you will first earn the money to buy it. If it isn't important enough to you, you won't!"

 Although it wasn't the easiest way to get a motor scooter, John understood exactly what his father was saying and agreed with him completely. I asked John if he ever bought the scooter. "Absolutely! But since that time, except for real estate transactions, I have never borrowed money to buy things I want. Not for cars, vacations...you name it! I always earn the money first. His advice made a great impression on me."

 "But I can tell you about the time I didn't take my father's advice; it almost cost me a great deal of money." John says. "He always believed it was a bad idea to give someone an option to buy. If you are offered an option to buy, take it, but never give an option. Well, I leased a restaurant building I owned and gave the tenant an option to buy for $650,000. Almost from the minute

Developing Stories

I signed the agreement, I regretted the decision. Through an unlikely occurrence, I got a second chance. The road in front of the restaurant required major reconstruction and was shut down by the city for several weeks. Business for the tenant slowed down considerably, and he asked to be released from the lease agreement. He was only interested in the business itself, not the real estate. We voided the lease, I marketed the property for sale, and sold it two months later for $1 million dollars."

GET A HOBBY: John's most profitable venture came as a result of his value for health, not wealth. Emphasizing good health is important enough to John that for 27 consecutive years he has made getting an annual physical a top priority. Twenty years ago, John's doctor told him that the absolute best thing he could do to stay healthy was to get a hobby. So John went and got a hobby.

Always a car enthusiast, John began to collect antique cars: 1959 Cadillacs to be exact.

"Why 1959 Cadillacs?" I asked.

"Because they are the most bizarre car ever made. Every year Cadillac would stretch to keep that image of success, and in 1959 they just crossed the line. Do you know the fins alone stand 4 feet off the ground!?" John laughs. "Eventually, I was up to about 17 cars and decided I had to build garages for each of them to keep them in good condition. As I was building the 10 x 20 foot garages, people kept approaching me asking if they could rent one. By the time I was finished I had all of the garages leased. I then decided to build 33 more garages for my cars and for anyone else who might come along to rent the extra units. I rented them all!"

Over the next few weeks, John traveled first to Florida, and then all across the country researching various garage sites and designs, learning about site location, construction and management of storage garages. Since 1980, John Messmore has built over 10,000 units on 26 different sites. His collection of '59 Cadillacs became world class with at least one in every color, and in every style. He chose a good hobby.

Even John is amazed when he considers that, "The only reason I built those 10,000 units is because good health is so important to me."

In the late 1980's, John attended and was very impressed by courses given by famous author and speaker, Anthony Robbins. John attended all of the courses, became a trainer himself, and discovered that the best way to learn was to teach others. John is a big proponent of the idea that "it is not what happens to you, but how you respond" that is most important.

"Situations will change and a variety of challenges will continually present themselves. The ability to positively manage your life in any given situation is what we should all strive to develop," John says.

So, get yourself a hobby!

Developing Stories

YOU CAN ALWAYS DO WHAT YOU DO NOT WANT TO DO

Don Kelley was working at his job installing telephone lines for the phone company when he decided to go back to school, study real estate, and become an appraiser. Today, it would require an entire chapter of this book to list all of his awards and accomplishments as a top Realtor, appraiser, developer and benefactor of educational causes.

Don is known for his tremendous success, integrity and humor. An attorney once told me of the time he was at a closing with a dozen or so buyers, lenders, attorneys and title agents. He said, "You could cut the tension with a knife, when all of a sudden Don Kelley walked in the room and, within minutes, had everyone laughing and acting as if they were at their high school reunion."

Except for my mother and father, Don is the person who had the most positive influence on me as a teenager and young adult. You can imagine how fortunate I felt to be included in discussions with him, his wife Nancy, and their family on topics ranging from philosophy and religion to business and poli-

Walking and Talking

tics. I learned a lot of valuable lessons.

I will never forget the lesson I learned regarding both the importance of, and the simplicity of, using square footage in the evaluation of real estate. Don mentioned that he had appraised a prestigious high-rise office building. I said, "That must be an extremely complicated process! I could never do that!"

Don answered, "Well, I met the property manager in the lobby of the building, and asked him how many square feet were on the first floor. I then rode the elevator to the top floor. I asked if all of the floors had the same square footage; they did. Then, I multiplied the number of floors by the square footage of each floor, and multiplied that by the price per square foot of comparable buildings that had sold. Always remember, Scanny, square footage never lies."

"That's it? That's all?!" I asked. I was astonished! Even I could do that!

"Well, there is a little bit more," he said. "I also provided information on the area and other supporting data, typed up a report about an inch thick, and charged $40 per ounce."

Of course, there was plenty more that went into that report. But it was his way of taking some of the mystery out of what seemed so complicated to me. He wanted me to think "that even I could do that," and he succeeded.

When I graduated from Miami University with a degree in marketing, I had no idea what to do next, and was open to suggestions. Don Kelley asked me what I would most like to do. I replied that while real estate interested me, it was a terrible time to get into the field. Interest rates were at 15%, the market was in a slump, and "salary" consisted of only straight commission. Everyone was saying that the timing for getting into real estate was terrible.

That wasn't Don Kelley's opinion. The eternal optimist, he said, "Sounds like a great time to learn the business so that you

Developing Stories

can take advantage of opportunities when the market comes back around." Then, he said something I will never forget. "Scanny, you can always do something you *do not* want to do, so why not first try something you *do* want to do. Think about it!"

It is wonderful advice for anyone considering which path to take.

Walking and Talking

GOOD ADVICE IS TIMELESS

Ultra-successful people like Don Kelley fascinate most of us. Don is one of the leading developers in the country. His most recent project, The Polaris Centers of Commerce, is one of the largest, most successful developments in the Midwest. We often look for traits, skills, talents, and work habits that people like Don possess, in hopes of emulating those characteristics for our own success. I believe I learned the true key to Don's success. It was the day he said, "Never underestimate enthusiasm. You can have the greatest idea in the world, but if you are not able to encourage and motivate others to join in, nothing will get accomplished." Don Kelley injects enthusiasm into everything he does and others respond accordingly. That is his key to success. So, how is he able to create such enthusiasm?

Don's enthusiasm comes from preparation. He first became an expert appraiser, which in turn helped him to recognize and evaluate real estate opportunities. He then willingly assumed the added responsibility and hard work of intimately learning every important thing there was to know about real estate.

A voracious reader, Don learned law, accounting, zoning

issues, financing and title issues as they pertained to real estate. He came to know as much as the attorneys, zoning officials, lenders and title officers. Although he surrounded himself with the most qualified experts, he did not allow his success to rely solely on their efforts and expertise. They were experts in their respective fields, but Don himself became an expert in every field concerning real estate matters.

As a result, everyone is on his turf, instead of the other way around. His knowledge instills confidence, which in turn creates the needed enthusiasm everyone wants to feel before moving forward on a project.

In putting together the stories for this book, I showed Don the story I wrote about him and asked exactly how he got his initial start in real estate. He told me something very interesting. In 1952, after serving in the Korean War, Don was on a ship returning to the States. A terrible bout of dysentery broke out on the ship and Don was one of the people given the responsibility of mopping up the unpleasant results. After hours of sickening work, Don took a break on deck and looked up to the top tiers of the ship.

"I couldn't believe it! There were actually people lounging on chairs, basking in the sun, sipping lemonade!" He said. "I later discovered that the only difference between those guys upstairs sipping lemonade and us guys doing the mopping was education. Right then and there, I promised myself I would enroll at The Ohio State University and get a college degree." (Maybe this helps explain the tremendous commitment Don gives to the education of young people in Ohio.)

After graduation, Don was quickly offered a managerial position with the phone company, supervising 30 people for a higher salary than he had ever earned in his life. But Don was much more interested in real estate. So he had an important decision to make!

Then, Don's uncle, John Kelley, told him something that Don never forgot. "Scanny, he told me exactly what you have written there that I told you. He told me I could always do what I didn't like to do, so why not instead try doing something I would like to do? That is exactly what I did! Isn't that something?!" Don laughed.

I never met John Kelley, but his influence continues to have a great impact. So pass on the word!

Developing Stories

GREEN ACRES

There is a limitless number of stories Don Kelley could tell from his long and successful career in real estate, but when asked to recall a story, the first one he thought of involved his business partner of over 35 years, Bob Weiler.

You are going to read more about Bob Weiler later, but first, let me give you some background. Besides being one of the Midwest's premier developers, Bob was named "Philanthropist of the Year" in Central Ohio in 2000. He is involved in every aspect of the community. The Robert Weiler Company, founded by Bob's father, recently celebrated its 75th year in business. (So long ago, that Bob's father once hesitated to lease restaurant space to McDonalds, because he didn't consider them to be a particularly good credit risk.) Bob is past president of the Columbus Board of Realtors and best friends with partner Don Kelley who rewards this friendship with the following story:

"We were in our late 20's to early 30's when Bob and I were given the contract to appraise a group of farms in Michigan. As young guys, we were excited to get the work. At the time, however, we didn't know much about farmland. We were city boys.

Walking and Talking

Bob was intent on learning everything there was to know about farmland. He collected and read all kinds of books and periodicals for information on farming, evaluating farms, etc."

Don continued, "You should have seen the skeptical look on the old farmer's face when the two of us drove up in our car to appraise his farm! But Bob was great. He asked how much pastureland the farmer owned, how much wasteland there was, and how much land was left for raising crops. Growing more confident with each question, Bob asked how many rods of fencing the farmer had and if the fencing around the cattle was electrified. I could tell the farmer was still a little skeptical, but I was very impressed."

"When we entered the barn, Bob reached down and sampled the soil back and forth in his hands then looked up and asked the farmer if he had adequate drainage tile throughout his property. The farmer replied that he had good drainage everywhere on his farm, but he looked puzzled. To change the subject, Bob asked, 'Is this silt loam or silt clay soil?' "

"The farmer looked Bob straight in the eye and answered, "Sonny, what you got there in your hand is cow #*%."

Don burst out laughing, which caused Bob to do the same. The farmer just shook his head at the city boys.

Green Acres Epilogue:

Since the previous story pokes a bit of fun at Bob, the first thing I did when I met with him was to ask him to read the final version of "Green Acres."

Bob laughed, and handed me back the story. "That's very funny," He said. "It's a great story...of course it never happened, but you go right ahead and tell it."

"Well, no," I said. "Not if it didn't happen! What do you mean?"

Developing Stories

Bob replied, "Years ago Don Kelley and I were in a continuing education class for appraisal and he heard that story and liked it so much, he started telling everyone that it was me. He's been telling people I did that for 20 years. Silt loam! I mean, how would I know anything about silt loam soil?"

Now you have to understand that Bob and Don have been partners and best friends for over 35 years, and both have a reputation for practical jokes. We both laughed that Don would perpetuate that story for two decades.

Or did he? The more I thought about it, the more I wondered. This much is true; either Don has given that story a life of its' own, or Bob knows exactly what silt loam soil is!

Walking and Talking

IF YOU DON'T BUY IT, I WILL

It seemed natural that the first story that came to Bob Weiler's mind was a lesson he learned many years ago from his father, who founded The Weiler Company in 1925.

Bob's father, while showing a property to a potential buyer, said, "This deal is so good, if you don't buy it I will!" The buyer replied, "Well then, you better get out your checkbook, because I am not going to buy it."

True to his word, Bob's father bought the property for $13,000. Three years later, he sold the same property for $9,000. "Dad used to say that was the last time he would use that line in a sale." Bob says with an affectionate laugh.

It was great to hear Bob reflect upon the successful career of his father, building beautiful homes in Bexley, Ohio, and then to talk about his son Skip's real estate career.

"Dad and I had similar temperaments when it came to selling," Bob says. "People walked into these big, expensive homes he was building with obvious concerns associated with a high price. Dad would say to them, 'This home is probably a little too large for you. Luxurious homes like this cost a little more;

the rooms are large and require a lot of new furniture. Maybe you ought to look for smaller, more economical homes.' The buyers would immediately insist that they could afford a luxurious home and would write a contract for the house."

Some people say this is an example of eliminating a valid objection. Actually, it is an example of shifting the burden of proof. For instance, let's say in the above example the buyers viewed the luxury home, then said, "This home is expensive. You're going to have to do a lot of talking to convince us that this home is worth so much more than the less expensive homes we could buy." The salesperson would have to spend the next hour trying to convince the "jury". Since Bob's father was first to point out that the luxurious home was expensive and that maybe they should look at cheaper homes, the task of finding reasons why the price of the luxury home was reasonable was left to the buyers.

In retrospect, the decision to buy was a good one for the buyers. Over the next few years their homes appreciated considerably and continue to increase in value every year.

Bob shared another example of this sales approach that he used himself. "One time our company was developing several hundred acres in Dublin, Ohio. We financed each subdivision with a different lender because no single lender wanted to assume the financial risk of the entire project. We had basically tapped all of the local resources in town (this was before streamlined financing from national resources was available), yet we wanted to continue developing more of the lots. We explained everything regarding the next subdivision to the lender. He responded that $12 million was a lot of money and wanted to know how we could insure his risk if he chose to put so many of his eggs into our one basket. He had several reservations and it was apparent he would not lend us all the money we needed."

Bob recalls, "When I suggested that we were excited about

the site and that it was too bad that his bank was just *not big enough* to handle such a large development, he shot up out of his chair. 'Oh, what the heck, I'll do it!' he said. It was fortunate for us that he agreed to lend the money because we were almost out of alternatives. It was also fortunate for him, because the subdivision became a tremendous success and the bank made a great profit."

Bob also believes that it is important to undersell expectations. He recalled a time the city had planned a huge summer event. City representatives were quoted in all of the newspapers that they expected to attract 1.6 million people. When only 800,000 people attended, everyone remarked that it was a failure! Had they given projections of 400,000, everyone would still be talking about what a wild success it was.

"When we borrow money for a housing development we underestimate projections. We might estimate sales of two lots per month, and if we sell four lots per month, the lenders are tremendously excited with the results and are more inclined to finance future deals. We had the reverse situation occur one time. Inflation was high, so in our proforma we gave annual appreciation projections of 8% to 10%. It created a terrible situation for us when our lofty projections were not achieved. Always undersell," Bob says.

Bob told another story that demonstrates how a person can add value to his efforts by redirecting people's perspectives. One day Bob Weiler and Don Kelley received a bill from their zoning attorney for $50,000! While Bob and Don considered him to be an outstanding zoning attorney, the price seemed extremely steep. So Bob and Don asked him how he had arrived at the billed amount.

The attorney replied that he got the zoning changed from farmland to 540 apartments plus 900 houses and he only charged them $25 per apartment and $30 per house. Bob laughs, "When he put it in those terms, it seemed like a very reasonable fee. The attorney had made the fee seem like a bargain!"

While reminiscing about these stories, Bob mentioned a phrase I came to hear so often from contributors to Walking and Talking: good fortune. "Good fortune has a lot to do with things. I feel like the most fortunate guy in the world for 2 reasons: I have so much fun at work I can't wait to get to the office each morning, and I enjoy my family so much I can't wait to go home each evening."

"TOMORROW MORNING, WAKE UP 20 YEARS FROM NOW"

"So, who do you suggest I work for?" I asked Don Kelley, after deciding to enter the field of real estate.

After careful consideration, he said, "Go see a guy by the name of Pat Grabill. He is a young broker working in Dublin who runs a small office with about nine or ten agents. He has a lot of energy and talent and he will make that office grow." These were the prophetic words of Don Kelley. Don insists that one of the most important things you must do to succeed in real estate is to project yourself 20 years into the future. Make your decisions today based upon how the world will be in 20 years. He gave that advice 20 years ago.

Patrick M. Grabill went on to grow his company into one of the most respected companies in the Midwest, consisting of 700 agents in 23 different offices in Greater Columbus. Pat, a past President of the Columbus Board of Realtors, is an organizational and creative genius. He is one of those guys you look at and wonder just how he makes it all happen. I believe I know his secret.

Developing Stories

Pat is an extraordinary delegator. As much as everyone tries to leverage him or herself by delegating work to others, very few can do it as effectively as Pat Grabill. Why? I believe Pat revealed the answer when he said, "I have always felt that I work for my employees, rather than the other way around." He runs his business with that thought in mind.

Pat takes a genuine interest in other people, gets to know them on a personal basis, and has the confidence to entrust them with a lot of authority. That is the secret of his ability to juggle so many balls at one time and still get so much accomplished. He surrounds himself with trustworthy, capable people, and then lets them do their thing!

The day I met Pat Grabill for my interview, I felt as if I knew absolutely nothing about real estate, about business, or about how to begin. I could immediately sense, however, that Pat was way ahead of the curve. He had so many ideas as to how his company and all of his agents were going to succeed, you couldn't help but get caught up in his enthusiasm.

Then he handed me a test.

"Just take it home and follow the instructions. All of my agents fill it out and we send it to a company that evaluates the results. It will help you and me determine your strengths and weaknesses," he said.

No pressure. To this day I have not told Pat how lackadaisical I was in filling out the test. I actually filled out part of it while playing poker with friends of mine. "What were these stupid psychological questions anyway? We never saw any of these in school," I remember thinking.

Over the next several months, I learned more from being in Pat's office while he fielded calls from clients than I could have learned from any business school. I saw Pat build friendships and professional relationships that continue to this day, and I learned his approach to advertising, communication, personal selling, planning and development.

After three months, I asked Pat if he received the results of my test. He said that he had and would make me a copy. A couple months later, I asked again and got the same response. When he realized my curiosity was not going to wane, he said, "To tell you the truth, Garry, the results were not very constructive. Basically, they considered you a "Do Not Hire." I only tell you this because you know I'm glad we hired you anyway." Ouch!

Fortunately, I had experienced some decent activity and had sold a couple of homes. But the idea was certainly not lost on me that the test results could have been a real obstacle if Pat had not been willing to take a chance on me.

Five years later, when I decided to specialize in investment real estate, Pat was very supportive and recommended me to Coldwell Banker Commercial Real Estate (now CB Richard Ellis). Bill Jones, their very popular Resident Manager, told me that my interviews had gone well, and that they would like me to take an all-day test. Oh no! Not again!

Bill set a time when I could meet with him and Chuck Manofsky to discuss the test results. I would find out whether or not they would hire me. In the event the news was bad, I was prepared. I planned to question their logic of deferring their personal opinion of my capabilities to the results of a test, graded by someone they did not even know. I wanted the job badly and was definitely on edge when I walked into Bill's office.

Bill said that the test results gave a recommendation to hire, and that they had decided to give me the job. He went on to say that the test results showed one characteristic that had been considered a 'concern' of the testers, a concern that he did not necessarily consider to be a negative. Bill said, "Garry, it indicates that you do not take criticism well."

Relieved that I had passed the test and been hired for the job I said, "I take great exception to that statement!"

For a second Bill and Chuck had that look of, "Whoa...maybe this guy does have a problem." I quickly laughed and told them I was just kidding.

But I would not have been laughing had Pat Grabill not decided to take a chance on me. The personal interest he took in my career is an example of the commitment he gives to others. This in turn results in the tremendous loyalty he receives from his agents, managers, lenders, attorneys, investors, architects, accountants, zoning officials, etc.

It is one thing to hear people talk about how important it is to be a people person. It is much more inspiring to actually see someone like Pat Grabill become ultra-successful by being one.

Today Pat Grabill is involved in real estate on many different levels. However, he is currently taking advantage of current market conditions by converting high-end apartments into owner occupied condominiums. By maintaining personal relationships over the years, Pat is in a unique position to oversee that process on a grand scale.

Of course Don Kelley must have known all of this...20 years ago.

EMERGENCY PHONE CALL!

Pat Grabill remembers exactly where he was the day his secretary gave him the message that Bob Weiler wanted Pat to call him as soon as possible! "Mr. Weiler says it is an emergency. It has to do with Hemingway Village, and he needs to talk to you right away!"

Hemingway Village was a new single-family home subdivision that Pat was marketing for Bob Weiler and Don Kelley. Because of a slow economy and 16 percent interest rates, the subdivision consisted of a handful of vacant "spec" houses scattered across 50 acres of vacant farmland and new roads built for traffic that never arrived. Hundreds of hours and thousands of dollars spent marketing the lots were no match for a down market. "And now Bob has an emergency of some kind," Pat thought as he dialed Bob's number.

"Pat!" Bob said. "We have a great new plan for Hemingway Village. This year we go from oats to rye!"

9

A Second Set of Footprints

Walking and Talking

A Second Set of Footprints

"I learned that hard work is an essential part of life - that by and large you don't get something for nothing - and that America was a place that offered unlimited opportunity to those who did work hard. I learned to admire risk takers and entrepreneurs, be they farmers or small merchants, who went to work and took small risks to build something for themselves and their children, pushing at the boundaries of their lives to make them better."

Ronald Reagan from An American Life

 Set of Footsteps** consists of stories from those
ors who are 2nd or 3rd generation real estate
ls, and of those who paved the way for them to
he world of real estate it is prevalent for a son or
follow the real estate footsteps of their parents,
e in sales, appraisal, development, lending,
itecture, etc.

e said, "Few things are harder to put up with
nple." Following are some good examples…

Walking and Talking

IT'S ALL ABOUT TIMING

Skip Weiler tells the story of his very first day in real estate. His father, Bob Weiler, and business partner Don Kelley were closing the sale of a large piece of land and Skip was sitting at the table ready to learn about real estate.

All of the closing statements, deeds and mortgages were signed and various checks were being distributed when Skip caught sight of the proceeds check for over one million dollars. Don Kelley noticed Skip's eyes light up at the sight of such a large sum of money.

Don said, "Skip, it is important you understand everything that was involved in getting this transaction to the closing table. Your father and I purchased this ground over 20 years ago. It took us 10 years to zone and develop the ground. Over the following 10 years, we had to sell off portions of the land to pay back various lenders. All of this took a lot of time and patience and also involved a great deal of risk."

Skip recounts today what he thought was on Don's mind. "Don was concerned that I would be left with unrealistic expectations; that real estate was all about sitting down at a clo

A Second Set of Footprints

and leaving with a big check, instead of working hard, maintaining discipline, and accepting risk."

Don continued, "Skip, it is all about timing in this business...timing!"

Skip listened and nodded, then announced, "Well Don, it looks like my timing is pretty good!"

Skip recalls another example of good timing involving a farmer who owned 80 acres in an emerging area of development. Skip predicted the ground would eventually tie in well with the nearby office and retail construction. Other land sites in the area had sold for 35 hundred per acre, so when the farmer quoted Skip a price of 22, Skip thought it was a good opportunity, even though the farmer's land was not quite as attractive as the other comparable land sales. After 8 months of working with the farmer and researching development possibilities with city officials, land planners and utility experts, Skip was surprised to discover that the farmer wanted 22 an acre all right. Twenty-two thousand that is!

The land was not worth anywhere near that amount. So the farmer did the next best thing. He waited five years, *then* sold it for twenty-two thousand per acre. It's all about timing.

Footnote: In 2004 Skip Weiler became the Columbus Board of Realtors® first 3rd generation president, following the footsteps of his grandfather (President '55) and father (President '76).

LET'S SKIP TO ANOTHER STORY

Some of the best lessons are learned from the shortest of stories. Skip Weiler recalls one of the first purchase contract offers he ever made: "I wrote an offer for a buyer interested in a four-family apartment building. To protect me, my attorney included dozens of conditions and contingencies to my puchase contract. The sellers accepted another offer and we lost out. My father took a look at the contract and explained that I had 15 different contingencies that were not necessary. The moral of the story is 'Do not negotiate for things that will never occur.' You can lose the deal or end up paying more for the property."

I couldn't agree more with Skip, or the advice I received one day from my mother. She said, "Before you ask a question, be sure you want to have an answer." I think of this every time an investor insists on having a seller quote a sales price before they will make an offer. I explain that the answer might end up costing them money. Here's why: When you insist the seller be the first to quote a price, it forces them to consider every sales aspect of their property. It is only natural that they will focus on those factors that favor a high price. Then of course they will

A Second Set of Footprints

add a "fudge factor" to the price in anticipation of negotiations back and forth.

One time, on behalf of a buyer, I asked a seller to quote a price on a property. Begrudgingly, the seller quoted a price that was entirely unrealistic. And from that point forward he considered his asking price "set in stone." Had the buyer made an offer before getting a quoted price from the seller, along with valid reasons justifying the price, there would have been a better chance of the two reaching an agreement.

Another lesson everyone in real estate discovers at one time or another is that you cannot judge a book by its cover. One time Skip was selling a building for half a million dollars. The person who showed up to look at the property had only half of his shirt tucked-in to a pair of blue jeans that appeared to have not been washed for a week. It was noon, yet it was obvious that the buyer had just rolled out of bed. Then he told Skip that he didn't have a job. Skip wasn't sure this was the best candidate to buy an office building, until he found out the person had just inherited over $50 million. He probably had enough money in his glove compartment to buy that building!

For some reason, Skip's story reminds me of the time a buyer showed up for a closing with his $34,000 down payment in cash! He said, "I am a cash-on-the-barrelhead type. Forget all these certified checks and wire transfers, or what have you. I deal in cold hard cash." The problem for the title company was that it was Friday, and they had to be responsible for all this cash over the weekend. It took five minutes to count out the money, and everyone groaned when the buyer was $300 short!

Walking and Talking

EIGHT IS ENOUGH

His last name is Kelley and he was born on St. Patrick's Day in 1960. If you guessed his parents named him Patrick, you are right. Pat Kelley is President of Falco, Smith & Kelley Ltd. But his real claim to fame is that he and his wife Lisa had a baby girl named Erin, then another girl Beth, then another girl Kate, then another girl Kara, then another girl Blaire, then another girl Mary, then another girl Abbie, and finally another girl Colleen. Boy! (Well, no, they didn't have a boy.) You can imagine, Pat stays extremely busy at home tending to the kids' activities, and at work earning income for all of those future weddings!

Pat was particularly pleased when a buyer came along to purchase the last remaining strip of land in a development being sold by Pat's company. It was a relatively small piece of land that had very limited use because there was a creek running straight through the middle.

Pat tells the story: "When the buyer paid us $75,000 for an acre of land with the creek cutting a path straight through the middle, we considered ourselves lucky to get such a great price."

A Second Set of Footprints

"So, after the closing, guess what this guy did?" Pat recalls. "He redirected the creek along one of the boundary lines! All of a sudden he had three developable pads. He built a car service center, a tire company and a self-serve car wash. For his final act he put up a billboard on the property!"

Pat laughs when he looks back on the buyer's ingenuity. Like everyone else, the buyer looked at the creek and thought it was in a bad spot. But it was his idea to make it run a different course, along the boundary. This enabled him to purchase the land at a discounted price.

According to Pat, "It just goes to show how difficult it is to visualize a piece of vacant land and decide how it can best be developed."

It was much easier for Pat and Lisa to decide that eight is enough. As for any more children, Pat remains very involved with helping The Salesian Boys and Girls Club in Columbus, Ohio.

THE-GET-RICH-SLOW METHOD

If you meet John Royer of Kohr Royer Griffith for breakfast at the Chef-O-Nette, be prepared for the waitress to ask him if he wants "the usual," and tell him to turn off his cell phone, because it will start ringing around 7:30 a.m. and never stop.

John is in his late 30's and his father, Dick Royer, has been selling, appraising, leasing and managing real estate for 25 years. Being around the business his entire life has provided John with many interesting insights.

According to John, "People who today own a lot of paid-off property, have been investing over a long period of time. To succeed in this business you have to live a long life!"

Investing in real estate is the get-rich-slow method of obtaining wealth. Sure, some people have created fortunes very quickly by seizing opportunities that others did not recognize, or by taking risks others were not willing to take. But most people who create wealth in real estate build up equity over several years of ownership.

What is the most exciting aspect of owning investment real estate? Insiders in the business will say the cash flow is impor-

A Second Set of Footprints

tant, and appreciation is great. But, most will agree that the great "secret" of owning real estate is that you are able to control a very large asset with a relatively small amount of money. Eventually, the large asset is paid off and begins generating tremendous cash flow. As John Royer so aptly states, "When you get to the back end of the amortization schedule of the loan, it starts to get very exciting."

With the discipline of patience and the blessing of a long life, many investors have created great wealth following the get-rich-slow method.

Walking and Talking

HE WAS EVICTED, TO HIS GOOD FORTUNE

While having breakfast with Ted Hobson, Senior Vice President of Carey/Falor Realty Partners, I asked him for an interesting story I could add to my book. Since he has known Wayne Harer for 15 years, I showed him Wayne's story, Walking and Talking, to give him an idea of what I was doing. He seemed to skim the story rather than read it.

"Scan, I don't have any good stories to tell," he said. Ted has been one of the leading office specialists in Columbus since the mid-80's, so I persisted, but to no avail. Sensing my frustration Ted said, "Look, if you ask me, Wayne's story says it all. There's no need to go any further."

"What are you talking about?" I asked.

"Walking and talking. I firmly believe that if a person does exactly what Wayne did, and still does by the way, get face to face with clients and know the product, they will be successful," Ted said emphatically.

I was surprised that Ted had actually read through the

A Second Set of Footprints

story, and said, "Yeah, Ted, that's great, but I still have 8 chapters to go!"

"Call my Dad. He's retired in Florida. He will have plenty of good stories," he said.

I made the call, and Gordon Hobson a.k.a. "Ted Sr." graciously agreed to give it some thought and mail me a story. The story began, "Boy, was I mad when the owner of a four-family apartment building evicted me!"

According to Ted Sr., years ago he was evicted from his apartment so that the landlord's son could live there. Ted's disappointment disappeared immediately upon discovering that an identical four-family apartment building, just a couple of blocks away, was for sale at a very low price. He purchased the property two weeks later, and within another two weeks he re-sold three of the apartments "with enough profit to provide a paid-off fourth apartment for myself."

At a time when many newspapers didn't even have an advertisement classification for "condominiums", Ted devoted himself full-time to finding similar opportunities to convert apartments into condominiums. With the help of partners, Ted converted and marketed over 1,400 apartments.

What a great example of opportunity presenting itself in the form of adversity. His eviction started a successful real estate career that ultimately led to his retirement in Florida. The weather in Florida that January day I spoke with Ted Sr. was 78 degrees and sunny.

COACH PEDON

In today's world of 24-hour news coverage, it is standard procedure for network news to keep a running camera on our President. They don't want to miss capturing the American President sneezing, or taking a swing and missing the golf ball, all those things that, given enough time and constant recording, will inevitably occur.

This obsession has spilled over to the American Parent. I am convinced that if little Brendan scores but one soccer goal in his otherwise non-illustrious school career, his parents will have video from four angles, as well as action photos, well before dinner. Even if the ball ricocheted off Brendan's hipbone past an unsuspecting goalie, the grandparents in Florida will find the video, in all its glory, attached to their e-mail hours later. When I was in grade school, the only "action" photo you got was the year-end team photo.

But, what if you were offered a one-minute video clip of any single episode in your childhood history? Would you pick the home run you hit, the race you won or the frog you ate on a

A Second Set of Footprints

dare? If I could choose one clip, it would be of an event involving Felix Pedon.

Coach Pedon was my eighth grade baseball, basketball and football coach. Tall, rugged and athletic, he took a real interest in every athlete he coached. He was a great role model who always insisted we give 110%. He worked hard at making us better ball players, and he inspired us to do our very best.

During one basketball game, Coach Pedon called a time-out. The other team was using a full court press to cut into our lead. A cross-court 'baseball' pass I had thrown was intercepted, which allowed them to score. In the team huddle, the last thing Coach Pedon said was, "And no more baseball passes!" He sent the message without singling me out. The very next play, trying to break their press, I again threw a baseball pass! Intercepted again! How could I have done that?

I was panicked to think the player would score again. I felt a huge surge of adrenaline as I chased towards their player going in for a lay-up. He missed. The next thing I knew, all 5 feet 2 inches of me was so far up in the air my hand was halfway up the net. I had never before even been able to touch the net! I grabbed the ball and spread my feet wide for a landing that felt like I had jumped off the roof of our garage!

I still remember the relief I felt at the next time-out, when I looked up and saw Coach Pedon smiling. "Well, I guess you made up for that mistake," he said.

If only I had a video clip!

One year later, Felix Pedon decided to sell residential real estate and became a top producer and sales manager for one of the largest firms in Ohio. His coaching, teaching and motivational skills along with his positive ties to the community helped make him a tremendous success.

Today, Felix is joined by his son, Chris Pedon, who majored in Real Estate Finance at OSU and has won numerous sales awards. When elected to the 2001 Governing Board of the Columbus Board of Realtors®, Chris was quoted as saying that he knew he wanted to be a Realtor® when "my father was chosen as the CBR Realtor® of the Year." What great steps to follow!

If you visit www.herrealtors.com. You will see that as a member of the management team, Felix's "sole purpose is to train, support and help sales associates reach their individual goals." Still coaching after all these years. Apparently, his youngest son, Ryan, is also coaching. He was recently named Assistant Men's Basketball Coach for Miami University.

It is good to know that there is a second generation of Coach Pedon.

A Second Set of Footprints

CHOICES MADE AND BIG SHOES TO FILL

Steve Falor had a difficult choice to make in 1982. An insurance agent for Marshall McClendon, one of the largest insurance companies in the world, Steve was offered a promotion to Wall Street in New York that included an increased salary, an expense account and company car; all the perks that go along with being given added responsibility within a large company.

And then he received another offer by a local development company, The Pickett Company, in Columbus, Ohio.

Steve had designed a comprehensive insurance program for the company and had a full understanding of their entire operation. He was impressed by the fact that it was a fully integrated development company, from in-house design and architectural expertise, to legal and accounting departments. Steve was offered the assignment of leasing their office parks.

"Our kids were young at the time and we didn't think the timing was right to pull them out of their school and move to New York. It would have required a lot of international travel

Walking and Talking

for me, which meant less time at home with the family," Steve says today.

Working for a developer provided Steve the opportunity to view real estate from the developer's perspective, while using his sales skills to lease space. His experience in the insurance business gave him a tremendous understanding of contracts because, as Steve says, "Insurance is basically all about contracts." He was well prepared to negotiate the lease agreements and purchase contracts.

Steve soon established himself as one of the most respected office brokers in Columbus. Three years later, when the Pickett Company turned their attention to developing hotels, Steve left the company to continue his specialty of office leasing, development and sales. In the last fifteen years Steve's annual volume has ranged between 15 and 55 million dollars. Today he is managing principal of The Columbus office of Colliers Company.

When asked about his success, Steve explains, "All sales come down to knowing and speaking the same language as the decision makers in your field. A drug company representative needs to be able to speak the medical language of the doctors and a brick manufacturer needs to speak in the same terms as a builder. Gaining the perspective and learning the language of the development side of real estate gave me an advantage in the tenant rep business that many of my competitors did not have."

None of this prepared him, however, for the day a buyer showed up late for a closing.

"The deal had been unusually long and drawn out. Finally, a closing had been scheduled. Everyone was there, the lender, the sellers, the attorneys for both sides, the Realtors and the title representatives...everyone except the buyer's wife. After an hour of waiting, we finally received word that she was on her way. Ten minutes later she walked into the room, wearing a

A Second Set of Footprints

yellow miniskirt, bright red high heeled pirate boots with fancy laces, a giant purple hat and sunglasses." Steve recalls. "She didn't say a single word. She slowly circled the table, full of some very upset people, and left the room. Never said a word. Everyone looked at each other in amazement. None of us could figure it out. The husband and the attorney went to find her. Fifteen minutes later, their attorney returned to say that we would not be closing that day, but assured us that if everyone returned the following day the transaction would certainly close. Everyone wanted to know what had happened. The attorney said that his client had determined that the aura in the room was not right. The aura! That really set people off. The closing took place the next day, so the aura must have improved!"

With all of the how-to books and tapes and newsletters that are on the market today, I was surprised by the number of contributors to this book who quoted their father when they were asked what was the best advice they had ever received. Steve quoted his father who stressed that if you always tell the truth, you never have to worry about what you say. Steve adds, "The three things you must have to be successful in any line of business are honesty, integrity and quality." Steve has made it a point to pass this message along to his son Doug Falor who, at age 27, has just completed his fourth year in the business.

"When he expressed an interest in real estate," Steve said, "I figured the best way to introduce him to the nature of commission sales was to have him pay for the required training courses with whatever leftover money he had from college. I try to be non-judgmental and take on the role of a guide he can consult with. He loves the business, is very competitive, and is doing very well. It is fun to watch him make his own way through this business."

Well, Steve, just make sure he schedules his closings when the aura is right!

Walking and Talking

10

Notes, Quotes and Asides

Walking and Talking

Notes, Quotes and Asides

"I really didn't say everything I said."
Yogi Berra

Following are **Notes Quotes and Asides** from the people walking and talking. Sometimes we gain a new insight from a quote that we read. More often, however, a good quote reminds us of something we already know. They remind us of valuable principles and successful strategies that have served us well in the past.

Walking and Talking

NOTES QUOTES AND ASIDES FROM THE PEOPLE WALKING AND TALKING

"Just as an aside, Scanny," Bob Weiler said, "if you develop land, you are usually better off if you sell the land to the end-user for less money and have them pay for the road. If you pay for the road and sell the developed land over time, at a higher price, you will have to pay the taxes on the gain immediately. But you are required to recoup the cost of the road over several years because it is a capital expenditure."

This is the kind of little "aside" that can potentially save you a lot of money some day. The lesson is to continually compare notes and share discussions with people related to your business. Experienced people like Bob Weiler can throw out "asides" all day that teach valuable lessons.

NOTES, QUOTES AND ASIDES FROM BOB WEILER:

Always remember the rule of 72's: Bob likes this rule-of-thumb of dividing 72 by the rate of return you are earning on your investment to determine how long it will take your investment to double. For example, if you are earning 10% on your money, it will take you 7.2 years to double your money (72/10). If you earn 8% it will take you 9 years to double your money (72/8).

There are more opportunities in real estate during bad times than in good times: "In good times everyone wants to buy real estate, so demand is higher than supply and that is reflected in higher prices. In bad times you can get some real bargains because there is less competition to buy. The stock market is the same way. However, when the market is down and prices are low nobody seems to want to buy. They only want to buy when everyone else is buying, when the market is on a roll and the prices are high!"

Crowded areas are a good thing: "Some owners and developers are fearful to own sites too close to busy areas, full of traffic jams that make it difficult for people to get to their location. I say bring on the congestion. People want to be where the action is, inconvenient or not. That's why restaurant owners seat people along the front window, and some even create a line at the door when they are not overly busy. They know that most people want to be with the crowd."

If you want to increase your calls from your "For Sale" sign, put up a "Sold" sign!: One time when Skip wasn't getting any calls off of a sign, Bob told him to try a "Sold" sign! "Every time we sell a building or land, everyone calls off of the "Sold" sign, wanting to know why we didn't give them a chance to buy it! We have had properties listed for over a year with very little interest...but once it sells, everyone in the world wants to buy it."

The biggest profit you can make in real estate is by changing its use: The single best way to make tremendous gains is to make a substantial use-change of the real estate. According to

Bob, "At Polaris Centers of Commerce, the land would only be worth $40,000 per acre had we not been able to get an interchange built at the site. The interchange changed the use from residential and multifamily, to office sites and a regional mall. Today, the land sells for between $500,000 and $1,000,000 per acre."

Bigger is not always better, but sometimes it is: "Many times, smaller projects are more profitable than larger projects. Other times, size is a great advantage. For instance, if the cost of extending a sewer to your site is $200,000, and you have 100 acres, that amounts to $2,000 per acre, which is affordable. But if you only have 10 acres, the cost per acre is $20,000 which is exorbitant," says Bob.

NOTES, QUOTES AND ASIDES FROM OTHER CONTRIBUTORS:

"Often times, the last people to find real estate prices have gone up are the real estate people." -Pat Grabill, citing how lenders, appraisers and real estate agents run the risk of not allowing the marketplace to determine value because they rely so heavily on comparable sales from the past to evaluate what the value is today.

"Real estate makes for the perfect investment. In stable times, it generates good cash flow, and in inflationary times, the cash flow is reduced but the property itself increases in value." -Don Kelley

"One of these days we will be the good old pros network." -Richard Schuen said this to me one day, years ago, when I blamed the "good old pros network" for my not getting a sale. I had complained that it was tough to crack into the group of

Notes, Quotes and Asides

decision-makers that controlled so much of the real estate activity. I will never forget Richard's response: "That is how it should be. Those people are just like you and me, except that they have been doing this for 20, 30, 40 years. They were building their relationships when you and I were in grade school. We are planting the seeds, and if we last long enough in this business, one of these days we will be the good old pros network."

"The best way to establish a relationship of trust between you and your clients is to get the decision-maker outside of the office, away from the stresses and distractions of the workplace." -Steve Falor, who considers his decision, early in his career, to use his credit card to replace a golf membership he had to leave behind when he changed companies, as one of the best investments he ever made.

"The key is to specialize." -Steve Falor

"Attitude." -John Beggs' answer to what he looks for when hiring employees (John currently employs 46 people). John strongly believes he "can teach all the skills needed to perform well, but a great attitude is something they either have or don't have. Attitude is second only to honesty."

"It just goes to show that sometimes you've got to go with the flow." -John Beggs as he recounted his experience in the 1997 World Skeet Shooting Championship. After shooting his first 50 shots without a miss, on a cold and windy day, he suddenly realized that he had forgotten to attach to his shotgun, a special weight, that he always used for the Doubles Event. With this realization, he missed his very next shot! (After regaining his concentration, John went on to win the championship with a score of 98 out of 100.)

"If you are going to burn bridges, you better be a good swimmer." -This advice John Beggs received from his father. "And in real estate that is very true." John adds. "Even when I differ with someone on an issue, I am never rude or disrespectful. I tell people it is like having a one-point advantage in a ballgame. There are so many close calls on a variety of issues, from zoning requests to lending concerns, that sometimes even a small advantage can be helpful to you. If you respect people and they like you, then the close calls will often go your way."

"Everything should be made as simple as possible." - John Messmore. As John explains, this doesn't mean that everything is simple. But you should work towards putting even the most complicated and complex matters into the most simplistic form possible. This is often difficult to do, which leads to another favorite quote John has on the subject: **"Simplicity is the hardest thing for a confused person to understand."**

"Those 20 minutes make all the difference." -Jim Garrett, who annually logs over 100,000 miles of flying, espousing the benefits of getting to the airport 75 minutes before the flight leaves. Before 9/11, it was Jim's experience that the rush of passengers typically began 55 minutes before boarding. "The extra 20 minutes gives you the chance to upgrade to first class, avoid the line, review your itinerary and grab a cup of coffee." How times have changed.

"One good investment is worth a lifetime of toil." -Don Kelley

Notes, Quotes and Asides

"Borrow long; lend short." - Stan Ackley. As Stan explains, "When you need money, lenders are scarce. When you don't need money, everyone in the world has money to lend. So borrow long; lend short. Time can heal a lot of wounds in this industry if you correctly structure the financing."

"One of my favorite quotes is that 'Life is too short,' because if you understand that it is not just a saying, but a reality, it can change the way you live your life."
- George Bakallis

"Sometime I see people in this business spending entirely too much time on preparing to do something and too little time just doing it. They are getting ready to get ready. Just do it!"
- Wayne Harer

"Never forget where you came from." - Don Kelley

Walking and Talking

AFTERWORD

Other than their sheer success, what do these winners in the real estate world of business have in common with each other? After observing their careers, listening to their stories, and discussing their perspectives on business and life, I came to this conclusion.

Each one of them is very good at creating structure in an otherwise very unstructured environment. Real estate is not your typical 9 to 5 job, where opportunities have been clearly identified and day-to-day responsibilities are well-defined. These individuals identify problems, needs, and opportunities and then set a plan of action that will provide solutions and fill voids in the marketplace. Step by step, they implement their plan over the course of weeks, months, and sometimes years. They are not told how they should allocate their time, or which deals they should pursue or ignore, or who they should include on their team of partners. For better or worse, they make the decisions. Their time and effort are always at risk, because typically any reward they earn from their work only occurs if their choices and decisions result in success. And the cost of failure is also theirs.

The characteristics they share include creativity, confidence, optimism and persistence. They demonstrate a willingness to make decisions and to incur risk. Not all were particularly good students in school, not all are consistently hard workers, and not all are exceptionally talented. But they all know how to teach themselves what they need to know to excel, can focus a lot of energy on important tasks at hand, and know how to work effectively with other people.

One of the dichotomies in real estate is that all of the successful people seem to succeed in very unique and different ways from each other. They all seem to take different paths, thereby taking advantage of their individual skills and talents. There is not one formula of success to follow, but hundreds. Because of this, it is almost impossible to predict, out of a group of newcomers to the world of real estate, which individuals will ultimately succeed. In essence the commonality among these high achievers is that they all take a unique approach to their business.

If lessons are to be learned from the contributors to Walking and Talking, they include surrounding yourself with good people, listening to good advice, adding prayer to your life, accepting the risks of the marketplace, understanding that success results more from being relationship-oriented than deal-oriented, taking a unique approach towards life and business that optimizes your personal talents, and keeping proper perspective on any resulting accomplishment.

Whatever journey you choose, keep walking and talking!

About the Author

Garrett Scanlon has represented buyers and sellers in the sale of over $350 million of investment real estate since 1990. A graduate of Miami University, Garrett began his career in real estate with Patrick M. Grabill & Co., Realtors in 1980. He joined Coldwell Banker Commercial Real Estate Services in 1986 where he specialized in investment real estate. Garrett joined Donald R. Kenney & Company Realtors as Sales Director in 1989. Today, he specializes in retail, multifamily and office investment property as president of Casto Investment Sales and also finds time to author articles, give seminars and teach continuing education classes on the subjects of real estate investment and stories from the world of business.

Garrett, his wife Sherri, and their two children, Michelle and Tony, reside in Upper Arlington, Ohio.

HOW TO CONTACT THE AUTHOR

Send correspondence to: Garrett Scanlon
c/o Ballylongford Books
2588 Welsford Road
Columbus, OH 43221
www.walkingandtalking.com

WALKING AND TALKING
57 STORIES OF SUCCESS AND HUMOR
IN THE REAL ESTATE WORLD OF BUSINESS

CONTRIBUTORS

Wayne Harer	Patrick M. Grabill	Donald W. Kelley
Robert Weiler	James E. Thomas	Felix Pedon
Bob and Dee Amsler	Donald Ray	John Messmore
Edmond Joseph	Richard Schuen	Bill Daniel
Skip Weiler	Steve Falor	Chuck Manofsky
Nancy Poss	Nicole Moore Wilcox	James Garrett
Cole G. Ellis	John Royer	Dave Fox
H. Roger Neal	Curt Arnspiger	Peter Coratola
George Bakallis	John Beggs	Chip Weiant
Kevin Clay	Patrick Kelley	Ted Hobson
Berne Bratys	Jean Snyder	Bill Owens
Bill Riat	Ron Moss	Stan Ackley
Bob Hoying	Brent Crawford	John Hall

Walking and Talking brings to life stories of humor, inspiration and insight from winners in today's real estate world of business. Top-producing sales agents and successful owners and developers share their stories with author Garrett K. Scanlon, a 25-year sales veteran of investment real estate.

A must-read for anyone wanting to gain added insight, from an insider's perspective, into the behavior, mindset and work ethic of outstanding achievers.

Walking and Talking's candid stories of successes gained and opportunities lost, capture the humor and enthusiasm of real-life people winning in today's business world.

You will laugh at and learn from these 57 quick and easy-to-read stories of creativity, hard work and good fortune!

Walking and Talking will leave you walking and talking too!

Walking and Talking